공항, 그 시절 인연
- Set It Free

공항, 그 시절 인연 - Set It Free

초판 1쇄 2025년 10월 27일
지은이 장선아
펴낸이 김영재
펴낸곳 책만드는집

주소 서울 마포구 양화로3길99, 4층(04022)
전화 3142-1585·6
팩스 336-8908
전자우편 chaekjip@naver.com
출판등록 1994년 1월 13일 제10-927호
ⓒ 장선아, 2025

* 이 책의 판권은 저작권자와 책만드는집에 있습니다.
  이 책 내용의 전부 또는 일부를 재사용하려면 양측의 동의를 받아야 합니다.
* 잘못 만들어진 책은 구입하신 서점에서 교환해드립니다.
* 이 책은 한국예술인복지재단의 지원금으로 출판되었습니다.

ISBN 978-89-7944-908-2 (03810)

공항, 그 시절 인연
-Set It Free

장선아 지음

The 3rd book of Poetry (by SunA, Jang)

The Airport,
Bonds
Beyond Measure

Sân bay, mối duyên thuở ấy

책만드는집

| 서문 |

 '시절 인연'이라는 말에는 시간의 강을 건너오며 스치고 머물렀던 수많은 얼굴과 순간들이 담겨 있습니다. 어떤 인연은 계절처럼 머물다가 떠났고, 어떤 인연은 오래도록 내 안에 남아 제 삶의 문장들 사이를 걸어 다닙니다.
 이 시편들은 잊으려 해도 잊히지 않는 이름, 멀리 있어도 결코 멀지 않은 감정, 그리고 나를 지나 나에게로 되돌아오는 여정에 대한 기록입니다.
 한국어와 영어로 쓰고 번역하며 저는 스스로의 기억을 이방인의 눈으로 다시 들여다보았습니다. 그건 단순한 언어의 전환이 아니라, 마음의 또 다른 결을 발견해 가는 여정이었습니다. 그 과정은 익숙한 슬픔을 새로운 언어로 다시 노래하는 일이었고, 그 노래가 때로는 저를, 때로는 누군가를 위로하길 바라는 일이었습니다.
 이 시집을 읽으시는 분들의 마음에도 지나간 계절의 향기, 다시 피어나는 인연 하나가 살포시 내려앉기를 바랍니다. 그리고 그 인연이 여러분의 오늘을 조금 더 따뜻하게 감싸주기를.

삶이 때로 버거울지라도 그 안에서 피어나는 아주 작은 따뜻함이 결국 우리를 다시 사람 곁에 서게 합니다. 이 시집이 누군가에게는 지나간 계절을 부드럽게 불러오고, 누군가에게는 지금 이 순간의 마음을 다독이는 조용한 쉼표가 되기를 바랍니다.

시간에게 시간을 주기로,

장선아 올림

| 프롤로그 |

2025년 사랑하는 엄마의 생신을 축하드리며

　더위가 절정에 오르면 나무에 꽃이 피는 하노이, 그 안 우리들의 공간 속에 친절한 그리움이 안착한다. 그 건강한 슬픔은 오랜 타국 생활 속에서 고국을 향해 자라난 것이리라.
　그 나라만의 상이한 질서의 담론에 적응해야 함에도 으레 고국의 향기를 쫓아가게 되기에 필자 역시 그러할 터이다. 어느 날 자리 잡고 앉아 한입 쏙- 그 시원함 속의 무언가가 뜨거운 감정을 불러일으켜 눈가에 이슬을 맺게 했다.
　동치미…… 필자의 모친은 먹음직스러운 크기의 무를 세상 가장 시원한 얼음과 어우러지게 하는 특별한 마법을 지닌 분이시다. 모친의 그리움이 투영된 그 동치미…… 이제는 함께 마주하고 웃으며 곁에 계셔주시는 부모님.

　가까스로 연결되어 가는 하루의 고리와 고리들의 이어짐은 세상에 대한 가치성을 이야기하고 싶어지게 한다. 무언가를 잃어버린 것 같다던 누군가의 토로처럼 세상이 쓰기에 한 잔의 목 넘김이 달 수밖에 없는 걸까?

푸르른 바다의 파도치는 소리 속 나를 다시 쓰고자 우리는 어딘가의 안락한 문을 열게 된다.

대한민국, 베트남, 다른 어느 나라에서든 귀한 시절과 인연들이 있다. 많은 것들이 계산으로 이루어지는 시대이기에 포용의 마음일수록 위로를 받을 수 있고 힘든 시간들을 슬기롭게 대처하며 오래 남을 수 있는 것이다. 그 시절들과 인연들, 시절 인연의 위로는 진흙 속에 피는 연꽃처럼 필자를 안아주었다. 이 책이 잠시나마 독자들에게 그런 안식처가 될 수 있다면…….

이 글을 다 읽으신 후 무엇을 하실 예정이신가요?
보고 싶은 분께 전화 한번 드려보시는 건 어떠신지요?

| 차례 |

4 • 서문
6 • 프롤로그

1부

14 • 쉼표
15 • 공항, 그 시절 인연
16 • 너울
17 • 꽃 샤워, 프리지어
18 • 에델바이스
20 • 봄날의 끝자락
21 • 다 지나갈 거야
22 • 시절 인연
24 • 문밖의 우연한 선물처럼
26 • 숨바꼭질
27 • 펼치기
28 • 집
29 • 개똥벌레, 사람
30 • 연리지 행보
32 • 자중자애
34 • 가장 조용한 언어
35 • 귀환
36 • 기억의 충언
38 • 시인의 자서전
39 • 시를 향한 기도

2부

42 • 하얀 아오자이에 꿰맨 저고리
44 • 갯배가 꿈꾸는 태극대교
46 • 울산함에 안착한 어미 고래의 포옹
48 • 국제 아리랑
50 • 우리는 지도를 함께 걸었다
51 • 어린 왕자를 비춰준 사막의 달
52 • 스파시바
54 • 두 개의 다른 왕관, 코로나

56 • 포스트 코로나이즘
58 • 파편의 정화

3부

60 • 어렵다 그러나 사랑한다
62 • 스피닝, 페달 위의 하루들
64 • 온도 1
65 • 온도 2
66 • 늦은 밤 태양 대신
68 • 낡은 앨범 첫 장,
69 • 생각다리 건너 등대로
70 • 희로애락의 휴가
72 • 인형극
74 • 최면
75 • 잃어버린 별똥별
76 • 고해
77 • 그루터기에 앉아
78 • 한강 작가
79 • 인사이드 아웃
80 • 너를 위한 노래
82 • 희망한다
84 • 조용히, 비엔나
85 • 중용의 평화
86 • 뜨거운 거 말고 따뜻한 거

87 • 해설_ 이승하
103 • 영어 감수 후기_ 조너선 셰린
105 • 베트남어 감수 후기_ 레휘 콰

영어 편

- 108 · Preface
- 110 · Prologue

Part 1

- 114 · Comma
- 116 · The Airport, Bonds Beyond Measure
- 118 · Swell
- 120 · Flower Shower, Freesia
- 121 · Edelweiss
- 122 · At the Edge of Spring
- 123 · This Too Shall Pass
- 124 · Bonds Beyond Measure
- 126 · Like a Serendipitous Gift Outside the Door
- 128 · Hide and Seek
- 129 · Unfolding
- 130 · Home
- 132 · Firefly, Human
- 134 · Steps of Entwined Trees
- 136 · Self-Respect, Self-Compassion
- 138 · The Quietest Language
- 139 · Return
- 140 · Testimony of Memory
- 142 · Autobiography of a Poet
- 143 · A Prayer Toward Poetry

Part 2

- 146 · A Jeogori Stitched into a White Áo Dài
- 148 · The Ferry Dreams of the Taegeuk Bridge
- 150 · The Embrace of a Mother Whale Anchored on the ROKS Ulsan
- 152 · International Arirang
- 153 · We Walked the Map Together
- 154 · The Desert Moon That Reflected the Little Prince
- 156 · Spasiba(Спасибо)

- 158 • Two Crowns, Corona
- 160 • Post Coronaism
- 162 • The Purification of Fragments

Part 3

- 166 • It's Hard, but I Love You
- 168 • Indoor Cycling: Days on the Pedals
- 170 • Temperature I
- 171 • Temperature II
- 172 • In the Late Night, Instead of the Sun
- 174 • The First Page of an Old Album
- 176 • Across the Thought-Bridge, Toward the Lighthouse
- 178 • A Holiday from Joy, Anger, Sorrow, and Delight
- 180 • Puppet Show
- 183 • Hypnosis
- 184 • The Lost Shooting Star
- 185 • Confession
- 186 • Sitting on the Stump
- 188 • Han Kang author
- 190 • Inside Out
- 192 • A Song for You
- 194 • I Hope
- 196 • Softly, Vienna
- 198 • Peace of the Golden Mean
- 200 • Not What's Hot, But What's Warm

- 202 • Commentary_ Lee Seungha
- 221 • English Editing Review_ Jonathan Sheerin

227 • Lời nói đầu

230 • Áo dài trắng vá Jeogori
232 • Dấu lặng
234 • Sân bay, Thời gian, Nhân duyên
236 • Thời gian, Nhân duyên
238 • Rồi mọi chuyện sẽ qua

239 • Đánh giá hiệu đính tiếng Việt_ Lê Huy Khoa

1부

그 시절, 인연은
출국장 어느 문턱에 머물다
비행기 이륙 소리에 묻혀간다
손에 쥔 비행기 티켓처럼
모든 것이 한 장의 여정이었다

잊기 위한 떠남이
이제 남은 귀함에 대해
더 사랑하게 되었다

쉼표

삶의 깊이가 녹록한 이에게
속 것을 투명화시키지 말 것을

마음으로 이어진 입김으로
불어 넣은
창문에 새겨진 약속들은
처마 자락에 간신히 매달렸던
물방울에 지워지고

혹은 가까스로
자국이 남아
귀한 형태의 관계를
띄운다

이분법적인 것이 어디 있겠나
좋다가도 슬퍼지고
슬퍼지다가도 미소가 되니

잃어버린 추억을 더듬는 밤이 좋아진다
마음의 객관화로 정갈한 시선들이
정리되어 간다

빗소리가 창가에 앉아 토독 깨운다.

공항, 그 시절 인연

창문 너머 활주로 끝,
익숙한 땅이 조금씩 멀어진다
가방엔 오래된 안녕과
마음엔 아직 끝나지 않은 이야기

그 시절, 인연은
출국장 어느 문턱에 머물다
비행기 이륙 소리에 묻혀간다
손에 쥔 비행기 티켓처럼
모든 것이 한 장의 여정이었다

창공을 나는 비행기처럼
나는 나를 데리고
나의 손을 잡는다

뒤돌아 바라본
공항 유리벽 너머
투명한 유리의 내가
다음 하늘을 기약한다

잊기 위한 떠남이
이제 남은 귀함에 대해
더 사랑하게 되었다.

너울

바람 한 줄기 스치자
강물은 조용히 떨었다
유리컵 속에 녹은 얼음이
강물 속 반짝임을 닮았고
나는 맥주 한 모금에
너의 안부를 적신다

도심 끝, 강변에 닿아
멀어지는 도시의 소음
가까워지는 심장의 박동

줄을 쥔 손끝에
속도와 자유가 묶여 있다
수상스키 바닥에 남은 발자국처럼
너는 내 기억에 눌러앉아 있고
강 너울 위로 번지는 노을처럼
나는 오늘 너를 흘려보내려 한다

강 울은 쪼개지고
햇살은 물방울로 흩어진다

시간에게 시간을 주었다.

꽃 샤워, 프리지어

밝은 빛일수록 그림자는 짙다
허나, 결국 시작과 귀결은 우리네들이었다
12월 연말, 다음 해에 희망을 꿈꾸게
1월 맞이하며 다시금 다짐을
2월 또 다른 새해로 재정비해도
3월 새로운 학기, 출발의 선상에서

새로운 시작을 응원해 주는
프리지어가 함박 만개해 있다
노란 향연들, 추위를 뒤로하고
따스한 꽃 햇살로 샤워하게 해준다

매달 그렇게 새로운 달들이 선사해 주는
희망의 그림자들은
먼저 봄이 되었다.

에델바이스

너는 피었지
땅 한번 밟은 적 없는 얼굴로
작지만 흔들림 없이
세상을 다정히 바라보며

해도 너를 비추지 않고
달빛도 스쳐 지나갔으나
손 닿을 수 없는 고도에서
너는 눈처럼 피었고

세상은 거칠고
계절은 불확실해도
너는 너의 자리를 안다

누구에게 보여주지 않아도
스스로 피어나
한 송이 꽃으로도
온 산을 밝힐 수 있다는 것을

흔들리지 않았다
피지 말아야 할 이유보다
피어야만 했던 이유가

더 분명했기에

흙이 없어도 꽃이 될 수 있다.

봄날의 끝자락

꽃잎이 햇살에 지친 듯
고개를 떨군다

길고 긴 겨울을 지나
지친 여정이었으나
생명의 첫 손길처럼
따스하게 피어나기를
조용히, 그러나 확실하게

짙은 녹음의 성장처럼
그대와 나도 하나씩 자라가며

새싹이 잎이 되고
기억이 꿈이 되고
계절은 말없이 다음 장을 넘긴다

봄이 물러난 자리엔
여름이 조용히 발을 디딘다.

다 지나갈 거야

추억은 항상 눈물을 부른다
가까워질 시간보다
잃고 멀어질 시간이 더 많겠으나
시간을 줄다리기처럼 당겨
이 모든 것으로부터 자유로워져라

걸림돌들이 산적해 있으나,
마음을 지켜 걸어가다 보면
디딤돌의 손길이 속울음을 멈추게 해
우리가 할 수 있는 게 있지 않을까?

시간이 지나 좀 더 자란 당신이
해결해 낼 것이라는 걸.

시절 인연

거리와 시간은
관계의 본질과 무관하여
은근하게 쌓인 일부분, 한 부분
그리움을 배가하며 더해지네

사랑을 했던 친절한 그리움
사랑을 받았던 번외의 길
시선이 머무는 곳엔
평행선이 없는 잠깐의 여행지

쉽지 않은 여행에서
예쁘게 바라보는 시선과 언어로
동행하는 귀한 생방송
그리고 재방송

시간에 비례하지 않는 만남에
처음이란 미명하, 과했던 언어들은
화려한 선물의 포장지

반복된 재활용 사용의
셈을 줄인다 해도
유한을 저버린 숫자여도

무한에 찾아든 언어의 고아

남은 기억의 잔재,
그 안에서
작은 에너지 아끼며
안식년에 들어간다.

문밖의 우연한 선물처럼

나에게
혹은
그 누구에게
수많았던 별들의 마주침이

유.독.
그날은
특별했음을

그 많은 날들에
한 날이 바랐던
특별함처럼

왜 우리네들은
하얀 입만 가린 채
특별함에 게을렀던가

덜 채워진 여백을
채워감
결.국.

그 자리는 그 자리에 있던 것부터

대체되고
채워지고
채움받을 수 있기에

특별함은
대문 밖의 우연한 선물
그 방문의 노크가 주는
평범함

숨바꼭질

다시 밤이 오는 시간
타인이 된 너의 빈집 속으로 불안한
내 마음을 숨겨둔다

펼치기

바다를 헤엄쳐 하늘을 날아
펼쳐진 항로를 빛나는 햇살과 물결에
맡기며 전진

집

준비된 무지개 속 찾은
진달래꽃 오,
희망으로 잡으리라

조촐한 상처들은
굴곡의 방향을 바꾸어
변곡점 소망으로
음악을 풀어놓는다

도시 아파트 빛들을 따라 걷는 산책길
꽉 잡은 손이 아닌
꼬옥 포개 하나 된 손
불빛이 체온처럼 다감하다

소녀의 꿈을 담은
상냥한 마음으로
가을꽃과 마주한다

한발 내디딘 보금자리
이제 느린 여행을 마치고
집으로 들어간다.

개똥벌레, 사람

늦은 밤,
버스 안에서 흘러나온
개똥벌레의 속삭임

각기 쳐다보는
창문의 이야기들을 그려나간다
수많은 버스 속
보이는 투명함

투영된
응시된 건물
      사물
        사람들 속
그려나가는 외로운 이야기들에
입김을 분다

"나를 위해 한 번만
노래를 해주렴 – "
개똥벌레 앞
반딧불이 춤을 춘다

사람들의 악기
시의 음악에 맞춰.

연리지 행보

시간을 좁히고자 했던
재촉된 걸음
그 한 걸음 한 걸음에 대한
정의는
멈춤에서나 가능하다

이제야 잡을 수 있는 손
내 팔이 뻗을 만큼의 거리인지
혹은
다시 뛰어야 잡을 수 있는 손인지
뒤를 봐야 했다

너무나 애썼던 그 많은 날들에 대해
지나친 눈길로
젖지 않게 했다

지나치지 않는 손길에
더해지거나 덜해졌을 뿐
간헐적 공복
버겁던 빨간 신호도
적적한 허무의 적심이었다는

해석되지 않은 기분에
바라본 하늘에 질문을
던져본다
어떠한 키워드로 무언가를 조망한다는 건

누가 시인이 아니겠는가
자신의 삶 앞에서

자중자애 自重自愛

우리보다 빨리 걸어가고 있는
세속적인 이방인의 삶에서도
세상에 흘릴 눈물이 별로 없더라

많은 것들이 다 지나서 좋건만
이 작은 두 손의 거칠함으로
또 달려야 함에
좋은 만큼 고통이 너무 많이 보여도

기준에서 비롯된 장거리와 근거리의
고정관념이 무장해제가 되는 시점에
마주한다

소통이 되는 순간에
원하는 게 많아지나
나도 정답이 아니었을 수도

겨울잠을 자던 내 세포들이
태어난 날
결핍이란 미완성의 소중함이기에

삼라만상 사람도 심장의 중심에 서면

덧없이 좋은 것처럼
음률이 흐른다

준비되는 마음들이 시작될 때
행하면
될 거라 믿으며

외로움이 수반된
모든 것들에
깊은 포옹을 보낸다.

가장 조용한 언어

말로 다 할 수 없는 날엔
입술 대신
눈물이 먼저 말을 건넨다

그 어떤 말보다
조용하게
회복시키고자

귀환歸還

하루하루
위태하게 붙잡았던
실타래를 푸니

풀수록 더 엉키어 단단해진다
손톱의 끝이 부러져
틈을 벌리다

소리 없는 토함으로
이기고자 하나
숨 쉴 수 없는
호흡에 가득 고인
내 웅덩이

아직은 가슴에 남아
그의 작은 손길로
다시 힘을 얻는
아침에 동반된다

소통과 충돌 속에 변하는
우리네 마음이나
견디다 보면
이기는 것이다.

기억의 충언

아주 조금 문을 연 채
걸터앉은 봉놋방 문턱
내 심중心中이 하는 말을 경청하며
서로가 기억하는 시계의 방향이 달랐던
모든 것들에 눈을 감는다

기억이란 나중의 안전한 기약을
위한 생존이지만
그 기능을 상실하더라도
행복한 기억만으로도 살아진다

사람 냄새 담아내는 시 속 풍경화 삶이
참 좋다
책, 차, 술 한 잔 기울임

순수한 믿음의 효과가
내 심중에
플라세보Placebo 꿈을 입힌다

다가올 다음의 계절은
또 어떤 모습으로 그려질까

기
억
될
까.

시인의 자서전

미리내에 비친
풍요로운 별들의
풍미는 멈추어진
그들만의 리즈 시절

장기간 장거리로 걸어 나와
삼라만상 속
흩어진 가루 속
화석의 귀한 줄임말은
신기루가 아니었기에

고리타분한 정답일지언정
시작을 가능케 하는
낭만이기에

달빛이 비치는 밤
은하수에 기대
함축이 가려주는 마음을
옮기어
언어의 선물을
준비한다.

시를 향한 기도

길었던 시들이
두꺼운 옷들을
챙겨 입어
여름 해변을
걷고 있다

짧아진 내향들이
얇은 옷들로
바뀌어
가벼워진 발걸음으로
물장구친다

극한으로 와서야
풀리는 끈이 아닌
오랜 여정 속에서

마실 수 있는
잔잔한 물
한 모금이길.

2부

변해가는 것이 아닌
더 자기다워지는 의연한
위대한 동작으로
함께 추는 국제 아리랑

강은 흐르고
호수는 멈춘 것처럼
다시 돌아오는
아름다운 원형

하얀 아오자이에 꿰맨 저고리

텅 빈 공간 안에서
최소한의 가능성을 선사받을 수 있었다면
불안에서 나오는 소망은 이루어지지 않으나
절실한 기도는 절대 땅에 떨어지지 않기에
놓치고 왔던 것들에 손을 주춤한다

내려갔을 때 안도와
올라갈 때 안도가
마주한다
이야기를 나눈다
지난 시간들
앞의 시간들

같은 색이나 하늘은 바다가 되어
바다는 하늘이 할 수 없는
파도의 모습, 구름을 흉내
햇살 속 춤을 춘다

도망치듯 나왔던 그곳에
반색의 얼굴로 인사하며
봄에 첫눈을 맞이한다

그 시절 우리의 이야기
이제는 느긋이 앉아 날을 즐기며
고요할수록 밝아지는 것들에
하얀 이름들을 새긴다

그들이 토한 호흡과 이름에
오래된 일들이 기억된다.

갯배가 꿈꾸는 태극대교

속초의 갯배,
마주한 아바이들 한곳에
멈춘 시계는
현재를 살아가는 그들의
한목소리였다

12시 정오 전의
분초차 아끼며
의지依支하며
의지意志로 이겨낸 그곳에서
의자에 앉아
시계에 사계절을 맡긴다

아기가 노년을
맞이해야 함은
시간의 흐름에 따른
당연한 이치인 것을

인정하고 싶지 않았던
진리를
수용해야 함의 현실을
시간 위 흐름은

변화의 양상과
함께한다는 것을

잠시
그저 붙잡았던 것

붉은 설악대교 아래
떨구던 눈물
푸른 금강대교 위
꿈꾸던 눈빛

무궁화와 모란에 치장된
태극대교 안
아바이 품에 안긴 채.

울산함에 안착한 어미 고래의 포옹

포개진
아래의 아늑함과
위의 그리움은
늘 대기 상태

고동 소리의 깊은 울림은
바다에서의
외로운 결투를 신청한다

베일 듯한 파도의 날
뾰족한 가장자리에서 빛나던
어미 고래의 호흡, 그 물결 속에서
모두를 정지시킨다

새로운 생명들의 힘찬 뒤따름
아름드리 해송나무의 질서들은
그들을 위한 퍼즐 조각을 맞춰
거친 바위에 용을 앉힌다

용이 휘감아 인자한 이불에
속삭이던 자장가
긴 어둠의 터널을 지나

견뎌낸 훌륭한 안착을 펴내며
포개진 대기 상태의 스위치를 내린다

한차례 지난 소나기
다시 만난
빛나는 생명은
그 시간으로 다시
되돌아왔다.

국제 아리랑

둥근 지구 위
많은 발걸음들에
안전벨트를 맨다

명상에 빠지듯
찜질방 구운 계란
고운 색깔 익혀가네
마음속 노크하네

맛있어 웃고
노란색 예뻐 웃고
흰색 밝아
백의민족
아리랑 춤추네

그리웠던 한복의 품
국제 아리랑 품에 안겨
구운 계란 한입 베며
아쿠

연약함이 마모되어 사라지는 것은
보편적인 것임을

완벽하지 않은 우리네들이
서로 나누는 응시와 기대

변해가는 것이 아닌
더 자기다워지는 의연한
위대한 동작으로
함께 추는 국제 아리랑

강은 흐르고
호수는 멈춘 것처럼
다시 돌아오는
아름다운 원형

우리는 지도를 함께 걸었다

낯선 호주 하늘 아래
말보다 먼저
눈빛이 길을 열던 날들

지도는 접히고
시간은 흩어졌지만
그 시절 햇살은
여전히 가방 속에 묻혀 있었다

먼 계절이 다시
창밖으로 피어날 때
유럽의 바람을 손에 잡고
한국의 골목에 발걸음을 내디뎠다

행보가 더디어져도
들리지 않아도
아무 말 없이
너의 걸음이 나를 기다리고 있었다

같은 지도 위에 서로를 그리며
작은 이름을 새긴다.

어린 왕자를 비춰준 사막의 달

오아시스를 찾지 못한
목마른 코끼리
그늘진 모자 속으로 대신하나

모래언덕 가파른 어둠
지친 어린 왕자
반짝이는 별빛들로 의지하나

황량한 사막은 고요할 뿐이다
멀리서 지켜본 장미
자신의 꽃잎을 별똥별에게 띄워
사막에게 고한다

모래바람이 멈추어진 채
사막은 고요한 달을 비춘다
사막의 달에 비친 어린 왕자의 눈물은 오아시스가 되어
뱀의 허물에서 코끼리를 탄생시킨다

길들여 망각했던 꽃잎의 향기는
목적지 없이 떠났던 기나긴 여정 끝,
사막의 달 아래 축인 물 한 모금에
보이지 않는 기억들이 기록되어
별똥별을 탄다.

스파시바 спасибо

강에 반영된 지난
카레이스키의 눈물
그 넘침에 비옥한 평야의 산물이나
연해주에서 만난 발해는
검은 재의 형상

피의 연대는 한결같고 무궁한 법이나
북녘땅 하늘조차 날 수 없는
한반도의 섬은
시베리아 횡단열차를 방황케 한다

실크로드의 동맥에
반지는 언제 낄 수 있는가!

순환의 링으로
끼고자 대신한 반지는
화려한 가면의 치장으로
같은 표정을 입게 한다

사람 냄새가 그리운 이들의 부작용
작은 것에서 큰 것으로
큰 것에서 작은 것으로

끼워도 빼도
결국 크기가 차이인 것을

웃지 않았는가
미끄러운 원통 색감 위
좀 더 큰 반지를 끼고
함께 기차에 탑승하세.

두 개의 다른 왕관, 코로나

밥을 마시곤 했던
다람쥐들의 발걸음이
물을 머금게 한다

멕시코의 코로나Corona 맥주의
열정을 따라 하나!?
뜨겁다 못해 따가워
도는 지구로 어지러운 원형 속을 휘젓는
너희들의 속도가 버겁구나

코로나 맥주의 첫바퀴로
부드러운 딜레마
날아가 버리는구나

땅에서 분주한 행진들을
멈춘 다람쥐들이여!

날개 달고 어두운 터널 속
박쥐로 완전히 탈바꿈하며
성체成體, 聖體의 모든 뜻을
다 담을 것 같은가?!

양립할 수 없는 것들의 대치
참 애쓴다
꽉 찼기에 들을 수 있다
비어 있으니 하는 소리다

아직 봄이 오기엔 이른 듯하니
동면冬眠으로 돌아가
변온동물의 온기로
각자의 자리에서 봄을 기다려봄세

코로나, 왕관들의 대적
흑백 가면 뒤 물에 흘려보내고
진정한 연대
조약하세.

포스트 코로나이즘 Post-Coronaism
-후기 코로나시대

지구가 정전이 되었다
낡은 것들을 너무 끌어안고 있었나!
새로운 것들이 들어올 공간을 찾다
우리네 몸속으로 잠시 피난 온 건가!

깊은 외상적 상흔 큰 전환점
지구의 카르마인가!
요행만을 바랐던가!

많은 화면들이 나타내는 유한적 숫자들
무한한 체념이나
결여는 고난을 견딜 심중의 근육을 길러준다

흐린 구름의 잔상이나
한 치의 오차도 없이 흐르는
시간의 동등함은
마주하는 하늘과 바다의 푸르름을
일치시킬 것이다

시작에 비해 간결해진
마지막 순간
피난 온 먹구름은

간극을 확인할 터이다

애썼던 그 많은 날들에 대해
지나친 눈길로 젖지 않게
미소 가린 내 마스크를 벗게 한다

타지에서 받은 마음의 포옹으로
고국에서 흐르는 땅줄기를 대신해 주었던
붉은 금성홍기에게
노스텔지어를 기약하며
태극기 품에 안긴다

파편의 정화

어느 푸른 땅
얼룩덜룩 파편들이 날아와
참혹히 쓰러지는
지구의 씨앗들

부서지거나 깨어진
주위의 앙금
시들어가는 푸르름
꼬꾸라진 야생들의 울음

미국과 호주의 산들이
불같이 우네
아프리카에 넘쳐나는
못생긴 메뚜기 행진
지구의 울음이 곳곳에 퍼져
흰색 가면 쓰게 하네

찌꺼기 파편들
주워 모아 분리수거로
통일된 마음이나
잠시 거리를 두고
지구 숨 한 번 크게 쉬기로.

3부

짙은 녹음의 성장처럼
그대와 나도 하나씩 자라가며

새싹이 잎이 되고
기억이 꿈이 되고
계절은 말없이 다음 장을 넘긴다

시간이 지나 좀 더 자란 당신이
해결해 낼 것이라는 걸

어렵다 그러나 사랑한다

술이 주는 명확성에
마음 놓은 의존으로

밖으로 날아간 그 소리들
고인 물 속 하얀 방해꾼들을
사라지게 한다

안착된 언어들이
장착된 것같이
차분해진

알면 이해였으나
모르면 오해인

싱싱한 꽃 버티나
메말라 고개 숙여
산소의 숨을 내뱉는다

묻고 싶지 않으나
묻고픈 질문조차

무딘 가슴에 묻히고 싶다

열정의 방향을 잠시 거두고

소리 내지 않는 희로애락에
이제는
익숙해지기

스피닝, 페달 위의 하루들

허공을 달리는 바퀴,
검은 타이어 밑에
쌓인 피로가 으스러지고
온몸의 피가
새 길을 찾는다

빛나는 눈동자는 음악과 호흡을 타고
자전거의 속도에 몸을 싣고
페달에 오늘을 얹는다
모두가 일상의 전사

거울 너머 내가 보인다
지친 얼굴, 붉은 숨,
그러나 포기하지 않는 눈빛
오늘도 나를 넘어섰다

삐걱이는 기계음 사이로
내면의 침묵이 깨어나고
하루의 무게가 천천히 내려앉는다
동작의 교감은
말없이 나눈 위로,
땀으로 엮은 연대

어려운 것들을 쉽게 풀어가며
각자의 밤으로 다시 돌아간다
조금 더 강해진 심장과
조금 더 가벼운 마음으로
기약의 일상을 뒤로하고.

온도 1

지상의 어둠 속 달빛인가
눈부신 햇살이기에
더 뜰 수 없는 아이러니인가

주차장의 형광등이 햇살 같아
바라보며 함께 끄덕인다
누군가 다가오면 켜지고
쉬기를 반복하는

외부의 들림이 차단되는 이어폰
두 줄을 타고 올라오는
불빛이 체온처럼
또 하나의 나처럼
따스히 배어들어 간다.

온도 2

완전히 자유롭지 못한
안팎의 온도들
화상 혹은 동상의
변덕으로부터

점점 늘어나는
견뎌야 할 일들로부터
자유로워져라

있어도 없어도 되는 것들은
없어도 되는 것이다.

늦은 밤 태양 대신

시원한 목 넘김이 좋아
넘겼더니
마주한 응시 때문이었구나

외밤, 참 화려하구려
조명 탓이었으나
그대 목 넘김
다음 순서에 대한
선약이었구려

굴러가세
굴러가세
드러나는 컬러
빛나는 색감
그대 쫓아가고 있으니

어쩌나
그 한 바퀴 나도 한번 탐세

혹시 알까
내 - 그 빛 따라 빛날지

비록
저 달빛이 애써
따라 하는
태양 빛의 끝자락이더라도

함께
빛나고 있지 않은가
빛나지 않는 건
아무것도 없다.

낡은 앨범 첫 장,

마른땅 갈라진 곳에
땅벌레마냥
들어오고 나간다

움직임의 반복으로
영원을 쫓는
무중력 떠돌이
상이함에 마주할 것이니

많은 엉킴을 풀어야
한 줄이 나오듯

오해의 기억
분명한 사진
그 안에
정지된 시간

펼친 페이지에
숨겨왔던 그리움 쌓아놓기
돌보지 않아도
반짝이는 별처럼
그렇게 앉아 있구려.

생각다리 건너 등대로

둥근 큐브에 이어진 다리
뿜어 나오는 생각 관계가
되어가는 새 가치들이
생각의 큐브로 돌아 우리에게 안긴다

세상에 마이너스라는 건 원래 없다
더해져 가는, 입혀져 가는
큐브 각 칸의 되돌림은
어머니가 우리의 집이라는 거

고민이 많은 밤에도 별이 반짝여 주고
아침엔 햇살 비치니
완벽하지 않은 우리네들이 서로를 기대며
살아가는 우리 모두가 섬이다

그러나 그 모든 우리네 섬들은 바다 위
등대의 별빛을 따라 이어져 간다.

희로애락의 휴가

불멍하다가 본 하늘
갑작에 급작을 붙여
세상에 칠하나
시에 덧칠 못 해

내가 제일 싫어하는
　　　변명만 늘어놓음에
내게 사정이었던 것들이
네겐 변명이 되어버렸구나

가까스로
마스크로
가릴 수 있었던
눈물, 웃음

자존감이 낮은 상태에서
에너지를 쓰고
자신을 드러낸다는 건
참 어려운 일

모든 걸 가지려 하면
모든 걸 잃을 수 있기에

그저
이름 모를 그 깊은 명사에
널 안아

답을 구해
과거를 묻지 않기를
      묻게 되지 않기를
내음하며.

인형극

객관적 지표의 안정에 상이한 손동작
머리를 흔들며 꼭두각시 줄인형에
손을 오르고 내린다

춤이라 추고 있으나
변하지 않는 같은 표정은
상이한 마음에
위를 보나 내려야 한다

춤을 추고 있는 연결된 줄로 찾아간
나무 막대기가 쓴 안경
빛 투영에 비춰 만들어진 디자인의 생성에
역사를 풀칠한다

성장기마다 옷을 새로이 갈아입듯이
가장 좋은 것들을
삶으로 초대하고 환영한다

소원을 비는 건 열매를 맺는 것
나무 막대기 안경에 꼭두각시 인형
빛으로 샤워한다

우리를 기다리고 있는
여름의 화려한 외출, 새해가 시작되었다
뭉게구름 소복이 한 폭 내딛는
발걸음에 날개를 단다.

최면

조용한 새벽 꽃처럼
밤에 아침을 선사함은
의도된 희망이었다

조화가 생화를 대신할 수
없으나
같은 색감과 미소를 주듯

꽃을 건넨 손에
남은 잔향이
그려낸 꽃병의 꽃나비

날개 달아
새벽 지나 아침으로
날아가라.

잃어버린 별똥별

명료한 의미의 빛
상실되는 순간
빈 하늘에
흩어지는 언어들

들으려고 했던 정성과
공감의
별빛은

긴 꼬리를 문 채
별똥별 되어
쓰러지고 만다

같은 날
한 시간에
반짝이는

무언가가 되고 싶었던
빛나는 시간은

눈물보다 작은 빛으로
허공에 뜬다.

고해 苦海

조용한 밤 찾아온
눈물이란 손님을 맞이한다

나타나 흘러서 속 시원하니?
머금느라 힘들었지?

그래
널 받아들여
너도 흐르고
나도 흐르자

미안하다
뒤에서 널 안으며
속삭이다 그만 -

이 정적의 비가 되지 말자

그루터기에 앉아

재촉한 걸음들이 뒤로한
어느덧 놓쳐버려
순백이 되어버린 기억들

그 많던 전래 동화들은
어디 갔을까
가난한 바깥에 남루해진 안의 이야기들

이미 알고 있는 건 없으며
세상 당연하다는 것 또한
없다

격정적인 순간들은
많은 것들을 만나게 하나
다시
소유라 여겨 지나가다 쉬곤 했던
의자에
다시

밀어냈던 낡은 추억들이여
어떤 하루하루를 꾸려나가고 있니?

한강 韓江 작가

가끔 마실 왔는데
마을이 너무 북적거린다

숨차 헐레벌떡
내 친구 찾아왔는데
헐레벌떡 숨바꼭질한다

흥얼거리는 내 골목길
뒤로하고
반짝이는 조명 놀이에
태양보다 더 환한 빛에 놀라
나 숨는다

언젠가 조용한 달빛 드리울 때
노크 없이 내 친구 집
방문하기를

그래도
참 고맙다
그대가 있어
모두가 있어
서.

인사이드 아웃 Inside Out

정서를 침묵에 녹여
존재 자체
희미하게 만드니
존재 상실
더한 먹구름의 눈물이니

격정과 잔잔함 사이
모든 것들에 대한
예의와 공존을
내려놓아야 함에

공허한 눈빛은
신발을 신고
투명색 이동 수단을 타
노래 부른다

아무도 듣지 못할
들어서는 안 되는
귀한 표상들

그럼에도 불구하고
무척이나 빛났던
밤하늘

너를 위한 노래

잠시 가동을 꺼놓아도
꿈틀거리는 꿈은
세상 처음 만난 새싹처럼
설렐 뿐이다

꿈의 방향은 바뀌나
내쉰 숨 거두어
어미 손 처음 잡은 아기처럼
포근할 뿐이다

보이지 않는 뼈에서
생성된 혈액처럼
보이지 않지만 느껴지는
나침판의 모든 방향은
가리켜줄 터이다

시계의 힘찬 똑딱 소리가
그리 따라가
박수 쳐줄 터이다

누구나 할 수 있지만
아무나 할 수 없는

누구나 될 수 있지만
아무나 될 수 없는

잠시 시동만 켜놓은 가동
꿈꿀 수 있는 꿈은
세상과 만나
꿈꾸고픈 꿈에게
열쇠를 건넨다.

희망한다

가로대에 앉아 응시된
일련의 칸들 사이
품고 안는 사랑, 그 가슴으로
희망하나 상충된다

바람의 스침에 숨 쉬며
가슴이 가난하지 않은 풍요로움이나
너무 잘해주면 거짓이 있기에
그 여하如何에 백지수표를
내민 건 아닌지

절기를 아나
스스로를 먼저 체벌한다
변화를 꿈꾼다면
오직 자신이 바뀌어야 하므로

얕았을지도 모를 넓은 바다에서
좁지만 깊게
무척이나 조심스레
항해해 보는

경험을 늘려 몸이 기억하길

바란 내밀함이었으나
일련의 칸들이 사라진 시야
그의 어깨에 앉아
익숙한 소리에 두리번
희망하나 상충된다

알록달록 몸의 여운은
그저 들리는 소리에 두리번
다시 보이는 일련의 칸들.

조용히, 비엔나

처음엔
책상 하나, 칠판 하나 너머의 거리였다
아우성 소리는
마시던 비엔나커피에 머금고
청중의 시선들은
배움에 목말랐을 뿐

밤의 긴 울음의 여정을 마치고
아침 햇살 따라 웃으며 시작하던
반복의 시간들 위에
한 시선은
비엔나커피에 초콜릿을 두고 간다

소리 없이 울던 휴지들이
그것들을 닦고
침묵 속 다정한 미소로 다가간다
무언의 소리는
투명한 격려로
어깨에 손을 얹어준다

무언가 잃어버린 것을 다시 찾은 것처럼.

중용의 평화

다소 버거운
몸의 무게를 이끌고
낯설 정도로 익숙한 시야에
고정된다

1년이 이토록 짧은지를
6월을 맞이한 제자리에서 절감한다

통감痛感의 꿈놀이는
시소를 타며
오르락내리락
중용의 숨바꼭질을 하나

나와 함께 탄 시소
마주하나
떨구는 고개 속

전래를 지키고자
발끝을 곧게 뻗고자 하네
하부르타의 진리를
가슴에 안으려 하네.

뜨거운 거 말고 따뜻한 거

불안에서 나오는 소망은
이루어지기 어렵기에
무엇을 잡고
무엇을 놓아야 할지
루틴의 지속이다

텅 빈 페이지는 더 많은 가능성을 선사하는
백지 위의 놀이터이나
이미 새겨진 많은 이름들에
변하지 않으면 불안해한다

하지만 내가 힘내면 다 안심하기에
흐르는 빗물을 내 얼굴 위에 걷게 한다
시원하게 고인 보조개 굽이

회고를 거친 삶은 더 컬러풀해진다
흔한 게 오래가기에
뜨거운 거 말고 따뜻한 것으로

평안해진 예전의 꿈이 다시 묻는다

어떤 선택인지요?

| 해설 |

세계를 품에 안고 큰 시의 그림을 그리다

이승하 시인·중앙대 교수

　장선아 시인은 이 땅의 시인들 가운데 꽤 특이한 이력을 갖고 있다는 것을 먼저 얘기하고 싶다. 시인이 걸어온 삶의 무대가 한반도의 남쪽에 국한되어 있지 않았다는 것은 큰 장점일 수 있다. 대학교, 대학원에서 영문학과 국문학을 전공하고, 호주에서 공부하고 일하며 경험한 시간들 뒤로 단국대와 용인대 등에서 대학생들에게 토익TOEIC을 가르치기 시작했다. 2013년부터 각종 국제 문학 행사장에서 동시통역과 사회를 보며 행사를 진행했다. 한국문인협회 대외협력위원이며 국제PEN한국본부 경기지역위원회 사무국장으로 지낸 후, 삶의 무대가 베트남으로 4년 정도 옮겨진 적도 있었다. 한인 잡지《신짜오 베트남》기자로 일했으며, 베트남 하노이의 고등학교, 대학교, 가나다어학당에서 한국어를 가르쳤다. 코로나 사태가 오지 않았더라면 그곳에 더 오래 머물러 있었을 것이다.《다문화일보》에 영시를 연재했으며, 앞서 낸 시집도 이번 시집과 마찬가지로 한영 대역이었다.

시인의 이력을 해설의 첫머리에 이렇게 쓰는 이유가 있다. 장선아 시인의 시를 보다 쉽게 이해하려면 지나온 삶의 여정에 대한 고찰이 선행되어야 하기 때문이다.

일제강점기인 1938년이었다. 《사해공론四海公論》이란 잡지의 청탁을 받고 서정주는 「바다」라는 시를 써서 보냈다. 스물세 살 때였다. 식민지에서 태어난 지식인 청년은 친구와 후배들에게 이렇게 외쳤다. "애비를 잊어버려/ 에미를 잊어버려/ 형제와 친척과 동무를 잊어버려,/ 마지막 네 계집을 잊어버려,// 알래스카로 가라 아니 아라비아로 가라 아니 아메리카로 가라 아니 아프리카로 가라 아니 침몰하라. 침몰하라. 침몰하라!"고. 이 비좁은 한반도에서 속을 끓이지 말고 드넓은 세상으로 나아가 네 꿈을 펼쳐보라고 권유하고 있다. 서정주 시인이 노년에 들어 세계 일주 여행을 한 것도 젊은 날에 꿈을 이루지 못했던 한을 풀기 위해서가 아니었을까. 장선아 시인의 시를 보자.

    창문 너머 활주로 끝,
    익숙한 땅이 조금씩 멀어진다
    가방엔 오래된 안녕과
    마음엔 아직 끝나지 않은 이야기

    그 시절, 인연은
    출국장 어느 문턱에 머물다
    비행기 이륙 소리에 묻혀간다
    손에 쥔 비행기 티켓처럼

모든 것이 한 장의 여정이었다

창공을 나는 비행기처럼
나는 나를 데리고
나의 손을 잡는다

뒤돌아 바라본
공항 유리벽 너머
투명한 유리의 내가
다음 하늘을 기약한다

잊기 위한 떠남이
이제 남은 귀함에 대해
더 사랑하게 되었다.
　－「공항, 그 시절 인연」 전문

　비행기에 몸을 싣고 바다를 건너 해외여행을 다녀와 본 적이 있는 독자라면, 또 일정 기간 외국에 체류해 본 적이 있는 독자라면 이 시에 십분 공감할 것이다. 여권과 비행기 티켓 한 장에 내 미래의 운명이 걸려 있다. 미지의 세계에 가야만 하고 말도 잘 안 통하는 미지의 사람을 만나 대화를 해야 한다. "창공을 나는 비행기처럼/ 나는 나를 데리고/ 나의 손을 잡는다"는 것은 비행기를 탄 이상 내가 믿을 사람은 결국 나뿐이라는 뜻이다.
　해외여행을 해본 사람은 꿈이 생긴다. 그 언젠가 다시 비행기를 타고 미지의 세계에 나를 보내고픈 꿈이. 갔던 곳에 또 가보는 사람도 있고 매번 새로운 곳으로 가는 사람도 있는데 아무튼 해외로의 여행은 우리가 다람쥐 쳇바퀴 돌리는 듯한 일상의 삶으로부터 탈출할 수 있는 확실한 방법이다. 시인의 호주 시간은 이렇게 시로 형상화된다.

낯선 호주 하늘 아래
말보다 먼저
눈빛이 길을 열던 날들

지도는 접히고
시간은 흩어졌지만
그 시절 햇살은
여전히 가방 속에 묻혀 있었다

먼 계절이 다시
창밖으로 피어날 때
유럽의 바람을 손에 잡고
한국의 골목에 발걸음을 내디뎠다

행보가 더디어져도
들리지 않아도
아무 말 없이
너의 걸음이 나를 기다리고 있었다

> 같은 지도 위에 서로를 그리며
> 작은 이름을 새긴다.
> –「우리는 지도를 함께 걸었다」 전문

지구 거의 반대편에 있는 호주는 나라 자체가 대륙이다. 우리 대한민국은 대륙에 붙어 있는 자그마한 반도 국가인데 그나마 분단되어 절반도 채 가지 못한다. 영어를 쓰는 호주에 내렸을 때 용감하게 "말보다 먼저/ 눈빛이 길을 열던 날들"이었다.

어느덧 시인은 "유럽의 바람을 손에 잡고/ 한국의 골목에 발걸음을 내"딛기도 한다. "행보가 더디어져도/ 들리지 않아도/ 아무 말 없이/ 너의 걸음이 나를 기다리고 있었다"고 하니 지구촌에서 함께 살아가는 너와 나는 서로 힘이 되어줄 수 있는 관계의 큰 형상화이지 않을까. 이렇게 우리는 "같은 지도 위에 서로를 그리며/ 작은 이름을 새긴다."

이제 세계 어디를 가나 한국인 없는 곳이 없다. 그들이 이민 1세대이건 1.5세대이건 2세대이건 3세대이건 함께 부를 수 있는 노래가 있으니 민요 〈아리랑〉이다.

> 둥근 지구 위
> 많은 발걸음들에
> 안전벨트를 맨다
>
> (…중략…)
>
> 연약함이 마모되어 사라지는 것은

보편적인 것임을
완벽하지 않은 우리네들이
서로 나누는 응시와 기대

변해가는 것이 아닌
더 자기다워지는 의연한
위대한 동작으로
함께 추는 국제 아리랑

강은 흐르고
호수는 멈춘 것처럼
다시 돌아오는
아름다운 원형
　-「국제 아리랑」부분

　이제 아리랑은 한국인만 부를 수 있는 것이 아니다. 외국인들도 따라 부를 수 있는 국제적인 공감대가 형성되어 있는 노래다. "완벽하지 않은 우리네들이/ 서로 나누는 응시와 기대"이니 노래를 부르면서 이심전심 교감이 되는 것이다. "변해가는 것이 아닌/ 더 자기다워지는 의연한/ 위대한 동작으로/ 함께 추는 국제 아리랑"이니 우리만의 민요가 아니라 '국제 아리랑'이다.
　제목이 러시아어로 된 시가 있는데 두만강 한참 북쪽 지방 여행의 산물이 아닌가 한다. спасибо는 러시아 발음으로는 스파시바라고 발음하는데 감사하다는 뜻이다.

강에 반영된 지난
카레이스키의 눈물
그 넘침에 비옥한 평야의 산물이나
연해주에서 만난 발해는
검은 재의 형상

피의 연대는 한결같고 무궁한 법이나
북녘땅 하늘조차 날 수 없는
한반도의 섬은
시베리아 횡단열차를 방황케 한다

실크로드의 동맥에
반지는 언제 낄 수 있는가!

순환의 링으로
끼고자 대신한 반지는
화려한 가면의 치장으로
같은 표정을 입게 한다

사람 냄새가 그리운 이들의 부작용
작은 것에서 큰 것으로
큰 것에서 작은 것으로
끼워도 빼도
결국 크기가 차이인 것을

웃지 않았는가
미끄러운 원통 색감 위
좀 더 큰 반지를 끼고
함께 기차에 탑승하세.
　-「스파시바спасибо」전문

　아아, 우리는 언제쯤 부산을 출발지로 한 시베리아 횡단열차를 타볼 수 있으랴. 시인의 말마따나 "실크로드의 동맥에/ 반지는 언제 낄 수 있는가!" 발해는 우리 조상의 나라였는데, 연해주는 우리의 영토였는데, 혜초는 실크로드를 8세기에 답사했는데, 시인은 그 여행에서 카레이스키의 눈물을 보고 왔다. "좀 더 큰 반지를 끼고/ 함께 기차에 탑승하세"로 끝나는 이 시에서 해설자는 분단 극복과 통일 지향의 의지를 읽을 수 있었다.
　시인이 외국에서 생활하기도 하고, 외국 여행도 다녀보고, 또 한국인에게는 영어를, 외국인에게는 한국어를 가르치면서 더욱더 절실히 느끼게 된 것은 '한국'이다. 조국祖國이라고 해야 할지 모국母國이라고 해야 할지, 이 땅이 외국에 나가면 왜 그렇게 그리울까? 외국에 나가면 애국자가 된다고 하는데 빈말이 아니다. 한국에 돌아오면 모든 것이 정답게 느껴지고 마냥 편안하다. 그래서인지 분단 상황에 대해 다시금 뼈저리게 느끼게 된다.

　속초의 갯배,

마주한 아바이들 한곳에
멈춘 시계는
현재를 살아가는 그들의
한목소리였다

12시 정오 전의
분초차 아끼며
의지依支하며
의지意志로 이겨낸 그곳에서
의자에 앉아
시계에 사계절을 맡긴다

아기가 노년을
맞이해야 함은
시간의 흐름에 따른
당연한 이치인 것을
-「갯배가 꿈꾸는 태극대교」 전반부

  실향민, 즉 '38따라지'들은 남한 사회에 정착하는 것이 쉽지 않았다. 세상 어디를 가더라도 이주민들은 원주민들에게 배척을 당하게끔 되어 있다. 속초에 가서 갯배를 타본 적이 없는 분을 위해 짧게 설명을 한다.
  갯배는 속초시 청호동 아바이마을과 중앙동을 잇는 케이블 페리cable ferry, 즉 줄배의 일종이다. 속초시 아바이마을과 시내를 연결하는 나룻배인 것이다. 한국전쟁 때 피난을 온 함경도

출신 실향민들이 고향에 갈 수 없게 되자 속초에 함경도 실향민 마을을 조성했고 시내까지 이동하기 위해 만든 목선이다. 이 갯배가 생기기 전에는 속초 시내를 갈 때 돌아서 가야 했던 불편이 있었으나 갯배로 갈 경우 직선으로 이어지기 때문에 실향민들이 시내를 갈 때 아주 유용했다. 이용객 감소에 따른 경영난으로 마을 주민들이 운영을 포기하면서 작년 5월 1일자로 속초시시설관리공단이 5년간 운영을 맡게 됐다. 시인의 꿈이자 실향민들의 꿈을 이렇게 그리고 있다.

　　인정하고 싶지 않았던
　　진리를
　　수용해야 함의 현실을
　　시간 위 흐름은
　　변화의 양상과
　　함께한다는 것을

　　잠시
　　그저 붙잡았던 것

　　붉은 설악대교 아래
　　떨구던 눈물
　　푸른 금강대교 위
　　꿈꾸던 눈빛

　　무궁화와 모란에 치장된

태극대교 안

아바이 품에 안긴 채.

─「갯배가 꿈꾸는 태극대교」 후반부

외국 생활을 하다가 한국에 와서 갯배를 타보게 되었다면 분단 현실이 가슴을 더욱 따갑게 했을 것이다. 대한민국 여권이면 세계 어느 나라에도 갈 수 있는데, 오직 갈 수 없는 곳이 휴전선 북쪽이다. 만날 수 없는 그곳에 사는 부모 형제, 일가친척, 죽마고우, 소꿉친구……. 아바이 품에 안겨 잠들고 싶어 하는 이들에게 올리는 이 애가를 다른 나라 사람들은 이해하기 어려울 것이다.

시인의 베트남 체류 체험은 이런 시를 쓰게 한다.

텅 빈 공간 안에서
최소한의 가능성을 선사받을 수 있었다면
불안에서 나오는 소망은 이루어지지 않으나
절실한 기도는 절대 땅에 떨어지지 않기에
놓치고 왔던 것들에 손을 주춤한다

내려갔을 때 안도와
올라갈 때 안도가
마주한다
이야기를 나눈다
지난 시간들
앞의 시간들

(…중략…)

　그 시절 우리의 이야기
　이제는 느긋이 앉아 날을 즐기며
　고요할수록 밝아지는 것들에
　하얀 이름들을 새긴다
　―「하얀 아오자이에 꿰맨 저고리」부분

　한국과 베트남은 몇 년 동안 서로 총부리를 겨누었지만 1992년 수교를 통해 문호를 개방한 이후 수출 물량이 해마다 늘고 있다. 박항서 감독이 베트남 축구 대표팀을 5년 4개월 동안 감독하면서 두 나라 사이는 더욱 가까워졌다. "지난 시간들"은 어떻게 할 수가 없고 "앞의 시간들"이 중요하리라.

　한발 내디딘 보금자리
　이제 느린 여행을 마치고
　집으로 들어간다.
　―「집」끝 연

　다시 밤이 오는 시간
　타인이 된 너의 빈집 속으로 불안한
　내 마음을 숨겨둔다
　―「숨바꼭질」전문

> 우리보다 빨리 걸어가고 있는
> 세속적인 이방인의 삶에서도
> 세상에 흘릴 눈물이 별로 없더라
> ─「자중자애自重自愛」제1연

> 기억이란 나중의 안전한 기약을
> 위한 생존이지만
> 그 기능을 상실하더라도
> 행복한 기억만으로도 살아진다
> ─「기억의 충언」제2연

  시인은 그렇다. 오래전 일들이 기억의 회로에서 아주 선명히 떠오르는 체험을 하곤 한다. 장 시인은 한글을 가르치고 영어를 가르치면서 더욱 자신이 한국인임을 절감하게 되었을 것이다. 그런데 여행을 통한 몸의 이동이든 영혼의 편력이든지 간에 결국은 집으로 돌아가게 되어 있는 것이 인생이다. 다채로운 인생행로를 걷더라도 길의 끝은 언제나 집이다.
  이제 장선아 시인이 자신의 시 쓰는 행위에 대해 골똘히 생각해 본 적이 있기에 그와 관련된 시편을 살펴보고자 한다.

> 달빛이 비치는 밤
> 은하수에 기대
> 함축이 가려주는 마음을
> 옮기어
> 언어의 선물을

준비한다.
  -「시인의 자서전」끝 연

 이 시에서 가장 중요한 시어가 '함축含蓄'이다. 시는 곧 함축이라는 것이다. "달빛이 비치는 밤"이니 지구에서 보는 은하수는 그다지 뚜렷하지 않을 것이다. 하지만 어쩔 것인가. "함축이 가려주는 마음을/ 옮기어/ 언어의 선물을/ 준비한다"고 하니 앞으로 나올 제4시집도 기대를 해보리라.
 그런데 시인의 시에는 긴 시와 산문시가 없다. 그건 시정신의 산물이 아니라 산문정신의 산물이라고 생각하기 때문이다.

 길었던 시들이
 두꺼운 옷들을
 챙겨 입어
 여름 해변을
 걷고 있다

 짧아진 내향들이
 얇은 옷들로
 바뀌어
 가벼워진 발걸음으로
 물장구친다

 극한으로 와서야
 풀리는 끈이 아닌

오랜 여정 속에서

마실 수 있는
잔잔한 물
한 모금이길.
 -「시를 향한 기도」전문

 길었던 시들이 이제는 "두꺼운 옷들을/ 챙겨 입어/ 여름 해변을/ 걷고 있"으니 완전히 내용과 형식이 균형이 맞지 않는다. 그런 시들이 양산되고 있는 시대다. 이제 시인은 가벼워진 발걸음으로 물장구를 치기로 했다. 그래서 시가 "극한으로 와서야/ 풀리는 끈이 아닌/ 오랜 여정 속에서// 마실 수 있는/ 잔잔한 물/ 한 모금이길" 바라고 있다. 시의 기능이 여기에 있다고 생각하는 것이다. "누가 시인이 아니겠는가/ 자신의 삶 앞에서"(「연리지 행보」)라는 구절은 20년 동안 시를 써오면서 얻은 진리일 것이다. 시는 결국 '가장 조용한 언어'라고 생각하는데, 이 진리를 장선아 시인은 외국어와 한국어의 첨예한 접점에서 얻었을 것이다. 그리고 외국 여행과 체류 경험 속에서 얻었을 것이다.

말로 다 할 수 없는 날엔
입술 대신
눈물이 먼저 말을 건넨다

그 어떤 말보다

조용하게
　　회복시키고자
　　 -「가장 조용한 언어」전문

　등단 20년 만에 내는 제3시집으로 이제 몸도 마음도 정착했을 테니 또 다른 의미의 시들이 장마철 봇물 터지듯이 터져 나올 시인의 앞날을 큰 기대감을 갖고 지켜보고 싶다.

| 영어 감수 후기 |

문장 사이사이, 지워지지 않는 마음이 머물러

영어 번역 감수 조너선 셰린Jonathan Sheerin

시詩란, 우리의 마음과 정신, 그리고 영혼 속에 간직한 것들을 아름답게 탐색하는 여정이라 생각합니다. 인생 속에서는 수없이 많은 변화와 도전을 마주하게 되지만, 그 틈새마다 고요한 순간과 성찰, 그리고 깨달음도 존재합니다. 장 작가님의 세 번째 시집 『공항, 그 시절 인연』은 이러한 내면의 성찰과 보편적인 진실—사랑, 상실, 기억, 변화—을 정교하게 엮어 깊은 고찰의 순간과 소박하면서도 가슴을 울리는 관찰 사이를 우아하게 오갑니다.

장 작가님의 시가 특히 강렬하게 다가오는 이유는, 단순히 자신의 감정을 표현하는 데 그치지 않고, 독자 스스로의 마음과 기억, 꿈을 조심스레 들여다보게 만드는 힘이 있기 때문입니다. 그녀의 시는 우리를 조용한 사색의 공간으로 초대합니다. 때로는 사적이고, 때로는 광활하게 확장되며, 그러면서도 언제나 진심 어린 목소리를 간직하고 있습니다. 일상의 순간을 성스럽게 담아내는 그녀의 시에는, 분명 무언가 특별하고도 마법 같은 감정이 깃들어 있습니다.

그녀가 번역한 영어 시들을 함께 편집하며 더 많은 독자들이 한국 시의 감성적 깊이를 느낄 수 있게 되었으면 하고 생각했습니다. 장 작가님의 시는 단지 아름다운 문장에 머무르지 않고, 삶의 체험이 응축된 문학이기 때문입니다. 섬세하게 빚어지고, 아낌없이 나누어진 마음의 기록입니다.

그녀의 시를 따라가다 보면, 우리는 어느새 인생의 사계절과 기억의 울림, 그리고 시간이 지나도 이어지는 인연의 흐름 속으로 안내받게 됩니다. 작업을 진행하는 내내, 저 역시 제 나름의 여정을 걸었습니다. 그녀의 시는, 이성적이고 계산적인 세상 속에서도 열린 마음으로 삶을 마주하는 것의 중요성을 일깨워 주었습니다.

이렇듯 장 작가님은 시를 통해 말하고자 합니다. 은혜와 사랑, 그리고 희망은 추상적인 이상이 아니라, 우리 삶을 앞으로 나아가게 하는 실존하는 힘이라고, 아픔과 슬픔 속에서도 태양은 여전히 하늘 위에 떠 있고, 때론 행복을 선택하는 데에도 용기가 필요하다고 말입니다. 그녀의 시는 우리에게 속삭입니다. 상실이나 고독의 순간 속에서도 우리가 서로를 사랑할 수 있는 마음은 시간과 언어, 경험을 초월해 우리를 하나로 연결해 주는 가장 본질적인 힘이라고. 이것이야말로 그녀 시의 진정한 본질이라 생각합니다.

조용하지만 영원히 잊히지 않을 메시지,
우리는 모두 연결되어 있다는 그 따뜻한 진실을.
장 작가님의 시집을 함께 작업할 수 있었던 기회에 깊이 감사드립니다.

| 베트남어 감수 후기 |

베트남어 번역 감수 레휘 콰 Lê Huy Khoa

   베트남에서 학생들에게 한국어 강의를 하시며 선생님께서는 언제나 한국과 시에 대한 깊은 사랑을 간직하고 계셨습니다. 이제 그 사랑이 한 권의 시집으로 피어나, 독자들에게 언어의 섬세한 아름다움과 삶의 부드러운 여운을 전해주고 있습니다.
   이번 시집의 탄생은 단순한 출간을 넘어, 세상을 향한 선생님의 깊은 통찰과 따뜻한 마음을 보여주는 소중한 증거이기도 합니다. 세상을 이해와 사랑의 눈으로 바라보는 선생님의 시선이 고스란히 담겨 있습니다.
   때로는 산들바람처럼 부드럽고, 때로는 여름 소나기처럼 격정적인 감정들이 시마다 펼쳐집니다.
   각 시는 삶의 한 단면을 비추며 기쁨과 슬픔, 사랑, 그리고 마음속 깊은 갈등까지도 담아냅니다. 여기서 시는 단순한 글자가 아니라, 심장의 숨결이자 바쁜 삶 속에서 잠시 멈추어 자기 자신을 들여다본 이들에게 전하는 고백입니다.
   이 시들을 통해 독자 여러분이 공감과 위로를, 그리고 때로는 작은 빛 하나를 발견하시길 바랍니다.

영어 번역_장선아

영어 번역 감수_조너선 셰린Jonathan Sheerin
미국 미시간주립대학교 정치학 및 아시아학 전공
KIIP Level 5 고급 한국어 능력 보유
에듀럭스 컨설팅 영어 강사
홍익대학교 · 한양대학교 · 인덕대학교 등에서 OPIC 및 영어 강의

English Poem Editor_Jonathan Sheerin from the USA.
Graduated from Michigan State University
(Political Science / Asian Studies Specialization)
Level 5 KIIP(Korean Integration Program) Advanced Korean Language Skill
Edulux Consulting Company English Instructor
Hongik University, Hanyang University, Induk University OPIC, English Instructor

| Preface |

The words 'Bonds Beyond Measure 시절 인연(si-jeol in-yeon)' carry with them the faces and moments that brushed past or stayedas we crossed the river of time.

Some connections lingered like seasons—only to move on.

Others remain within, walking silently between the lines of my life.

These poems are records of names that refuse to fade, emotions that remain near no matter how far, and journeys that begin beyond me, yet always return to me.

Writing and translating between Korean and English, I looked at my memories through the lens of another tongue.

It was not just a linguistic shift, but a journey—of rediscovering the soul's hidden contours through the mirror of another tongue.

It was like singing a familiar sorrow in a new voice—a voice that,

I hoped, might offer comfort not only to myself, but to someone else along the way.

To you, who now hold these pages:
may a scent from a past season return to you,
may a forgotten bond resurface—unhurried and soft—
and may that gentle remembrance wrap itself around your present moment, like warmth that does not demand, but simply stays.

Even when life feels heavy, it is the small, quiet warmth that blooms within that brings us back beside one another.
May this collection gently recall a season long past for some,
and for others, offer a moment of calm—
a soft comma in the rhythm of the day.
Giving Time to Time,

with love, SunA Jang

| Prologue |

Celebrating My Beloved Mother's Birthday in 2025

When the heat reaches its peak, flowers bloom on the trees in Hanoi. Within that summer's stillness, a gentle longing settles in the space we shared. That quiet ache—so honest and healthy—perhaps reaches toward the homeland, now etched into the routines of a long life abroad.

Despite having to adapt to the discourse of a uniquely different order in that country, the familiar scent of home has a way of finding us. I, too, am not immune to its pull. One day, I sat in stillness, took a single bite—and suddenly, in that coolness, warmth welled up, leaving a soft mist in my eyes.

Dongchimi……. My mother possessed a special kind of magic—she could harmonize the crispest radish with the coldest ice in the world. That dongchimi, steeped in my longing for her, was more than just a taste. Now, my parents—who once lived in my yearning—sit beside me again, smiling.

In the delicate links that hold one day to the next, I find myself wanting to speak of life's worth. Perhaps, like someone who once confessed to feeling like they'd lost something, we all search for meaning—and in doing so, even a single sip of something bitter can turn sweet.

To rewrite ourselves amid the sounds of crashing waves, we instinctively reach for the comfort of a door left slightly ajar.

Whether in Korea, Vietnam, or some other corner of the world, there are sacred times and cherished people— seasons of life that become our quiet anchors.

In an era where so much is measured and calculated, it is precisely these expansive, embracing hearts that become a source of healing. By meeting such moments with grace, we allow them to stay with us. The comfort of past seasons and relationships—Bonds Beyond Measure is like a lotus blooming in the mud. If they embraced me once, then perhaps these words, too, can offer a moment of rest for someone else.

    So now, having read this piece—
    What will you do next?

    How about reaching out with a call to someone you miss?

Part 1

Those ties of time—
linger at the dawn of departure,
then vanish
under the roar of ascent.

Like the plane ticket in my hand,
everything was but a page of a journey.

The departure—home usually forgotten
has now
taught me to cherish
what remains—
and to love it all the more.

Comma

To those who find depth in life too easy,
do not make what's inside too transparent.

The breath that connected us through the heart,
etched promises on the window—
only to be erased
by a raindrop hanging by a thread
from the eaves.

And yet, sometimes,
a trace remains,
lifting the fragile shape
of what we once called a bond.

Is anything ever truly binary?
Joy turns into sorrow,
and sorrow, into a smile.

I've come to love nights
when I retrace forgotten memories.
Detached from emotion,
my mind settles

into clarity.

The rain sits by the window,
softly tapping me awake.

The Airport, Bonds Beyond Measure

Beyond the window, at the runway's end,
the familiar ground slowly fades.

In my bag, an old goodbye,
in my heart,
a story unfinished.

Those ties of time—
linger at the dawn of departure,
then vanish
under the roar of ascent.

Like the plane ticket in my hand,
everything was but a page of a journey.

Like the plane soaring through the sky,
I carry myself—
I hold my own hand.

Glancing back
through the airport glass wall,
my transparent reflection

promises the next sky to be.

The departure—home usually forgotten
has now
taught me to cherish
what remains—
and to love it all the more.

Swell

A gust of wind brushes past,
and the river quivers quietly.

Ice melting in a glass
mirrors the shimmer on the water.
I take a sip of beer,
and soak in the thought of you.

At the river's edge, where the city ends,
the noise fades,
and the heartbeat draws near.

In the hand that holds the rope,
speed and freedom are tangled.
Like footprints left from the water skis,
you settle
in the weight of my memory.

As the river's swell
melts into sunset,
I try, today,
to let you drift away.

The water divides.

Sunlight scatters like droplets.

I gave time

to time.

Flower Shower, Freesia

The brighter the light,
the deeper the shadow.
But always—
the beginning and the return
were ours.

December draws to a close,
and we dream of hope again.
In January, a promise renewed.
In February, another start.
March—
a line drawn for new beginnings.

Freesias bloom in full joy,
cheering us on.
A golden fragrance
bathing us in warm, petaled sunlight.

Every month, each new beginning casts
the softest shadows of hope.

Spring, before all else,
was already here.

Edelweiss

You bloomed—
a face that never once touched the earth,
small but unwavering,
gazing gently upon the world.

The sun did not shine on you,
the moonlight merely brushed past—
yet high in untouchable heights,
you bloomed like snow.

Though the world is harsh,
and the seasons uncertain,
you knew your place.

Even without showing yourself to anyone,
you blossomed on your own—
proving that a single flower
can light up an entire mountain.
You did not waver—
because the reason to bloom
was clearer than any reason not to.

Even without soil, one can be a flower.

At the Edge of Spring

The petals, weary from sunlight,
begin to bow their heads.

After a long, long winter,
and a tiring journey,
I wish to bloom again—
softly, but surely—
like the first warm reach of life.

Like deep green leaves
stretching into growth,
you and I each rise—
one step at a time.

Buds turn to leaves,
memories to dreams.
The season turns its page
without a word.

As spring steps back,
summer quietly
places its feet.

This Too Shall Pass

Memories
always bring tears.

Though we may drift apart more
than we draw near,
pull time forward like a sprint—
and be free from it all.

There are countless stumbling blocks,
but if you walk while protecting your heart,
stepping stones will reach for you,
and perhaps,
there is something still we can do.

In time,
the grown version of you
will find a way through.

Bonds Beyond Measure

Distance and time
are not the essence of connection.
Layers of fragments
multiply our longing.

Love—tender in its remembering.
Love received—on a road off the main path.
Where the gaze lingers,
we find fleeting places
where parallel lines cease to exist.

In journeys far from easy,
the view softened by kind eyes,
the language of presence—
a precious live broadcast,
and its quiet replay.

Encounters not measured by time—
Words once too much,
under the illusion of "first"—
wrapping paper for a gift too bright.

Even if we reduce

the repeated use of such wrappings,

and even if numbers betray their limits,

we become orphans

of language slipping toward the infinite.

The remnants of memory—

within them,

preserving small flickers of energy,

I step into a quiet sabbatical.

Like a Serendipitous Gift Outside the Door

To me—
or to someone else,
there were countless
collisions of stars.

But that day—
for some reason—
stood apart.

Like the specialness
a single day might long for
among so many ordinary ones.

Why were we so careless
with the extraordinary—
hiding behind masks
that covered only our mouths?

And yet,
the empty space, still incomplete,
is being filled.

And in the end—
what already stood in its place
can be replaced,
filled,
and received again.

Specialness—
like a spontaneous gift at your doorstep,
wrapped in the ordinary knock
of an unexpected visitor.

Hide and Seek

When night falls again,
Into the empty house where you've become a stranger,
I quietly hide
My anxious heart.

Unfolding

Swimming through oceans,
soaring through skies—
I entrust this open route
to sunlight and waves,
moving forward.

Home

Inside a waiting rainbow,
I find an azalea—
and hold it with hope.

Modest wounds
shift the curve of the path,
unfolding music
at the turning point of desire.

A walk tracing the glow
of city apartment lights.
Not hands tightly gripped,
but gently folded palms—
as one.
The lights feel tender,
like body warmth.

With a heart that once held
a young girl's dream,
I face autumn flowers.

One step into shelter,

after a long, slow journey,

I come home—

Firefly, Human

Late at night,
a song hums softly
from the bus speakers—
"Firefly…"

Each passenger's gaze
draws its own windowed story.
Countless buses,
each one transparent in its own way.

Reflected
gazing buildings,
objects,
people—
in their solitude,
I blow warm breath
into the fragile sketches they become.

"Just once,
sing for me…"
Before the humble firefly,
a dance of light

from a glowing friend begins.

Human instruments
playing to the music of poetry.

Steps of Entwined Trees

Rushed steps
meant to shorten time—
but the meaning of each one
is only revealed
in stillness.

Is the hand now within reach
close enough to grasp?
Or must I run again
to catch it?
I had to look back.

To all those days I tried too hard,
I gave only a passing glance—
so they would not be soaked
in regret.

The touch that didn't pass me by—
whether it gave more or took less—
was just part of this
intermittent emptiness.

Even the overwhelming red lights
were the damp core
of quiet desolation.

In feelings yet undefined,
I lift my eyes to the sky
and cast my question.

To name something with a keyword—
isn't that what poets do?
Before the altar
of their own lives.

Self-Respect, Self-Compassion

Even in the worldly life
Of strangers walking ahead of us,
There seemed to be few tears left to shed.

It would be enough
to have moved beyond so much—
and yet, these rough hands
must keep running.
Even when joy shines bright,
it reveals too many forms of pain.

At the point where
fixed ideas of nearness and distance collapse,
I stand—
bare, questioning.

In the moment of true connection,
desire multiplies.
Perhaps I, too,
was never the answer.

On the day

my hibernating cells were born anew,
I realized:
lack itself holds
the fragile weight of something precious.

When people stand
at the center of the heart,
all things—like music—
flow without need for reason.

When a prepared heart begins,
action follows,
and belief blooms.

To all that comes
with a shade of loneliness,
I send a deep embrace.

The Quietest Language

On days when words fall short,
Tears speak first,
In place of lips.

More quietly
Than any words,
They seek to heal.

Return

Day by day,
I clung to threads
of unraveling life.

But the more I unravel,
the tighter it tangles—
until my fingernails break
trying to pry it open.

I want to win
with a silent surrender.
Yet I find myself breathless,
my chest filled with a still pool of me.

Still,
what lingers in the heart—
revived by the gentlest touch—
guides me into morning.

Our hearts—
ever shifting between communication and collision—
will, if endured, endure.

Testimony of Memory

With the door barely open,
I sit on the threshold
of the boiler room—
listening closely
to what my heart whispers.

We once turned
our clocks in opposite directions.
I close my eyes
to all that was.

Memory may be
A survival mechanism
For the assurance of a safe future.
Even if that function fades,
One can still live
On happy memories alone.

Life, captured in poems
that smell of people—
a painted landscape I cherish.
Books, tea, a glass of wine.

The gentle effect
of pure belief
lays a placebo dream
across the surface of my heart.

What shape
will the next season take?

Will it be—
remembered?

Autobiography of a Poet

In the milky way's reflection,
the flavor of abundant stars
lingers—
a still frame of their golden days.

Walking far and long,
through the scattered dust
of this vast world,
I found that the rare fossils
were never mirages.

Though the answers may feel dated,
they are romantic still—
for they make beginnings possible.

On a night lit by moonlight,
Leaning on the Milky Way,
She transfers the heart
That concealment through implication veils,
And prepares
A gift of language.

A Prayer Toward Poetry

Long poems
Layered in thick clothes,
Now walk
The summer shore.

Shortened lines
Changed into light garments,
Now splash about
With buoyant steps.

Not the kind of knot
Unraveled by extreme pressure,
But rather—

A sip of still water
Drawn from a long journey—
That is the wish.

Part 2

Not a matter of change,
but a deepening authenticity—
to be ourselves.
a dignified, majestic movement,
the "International Arirang" we dance together.

As rivers flow
and lakes remain still,
the beautiful circle of life
unfolds once more.

A Jeogori Stitched into a White Áo Dài

In an Empty Space
Had there been even the slightest possibility granted,
Though hopes born of anxiety may not come true,
An earnest prayer never falls to the ground.
Thus, the hand hesitates over what was left behind.

Relief upon descent
And relief upon ascent
They meet,
They speak—
Of times past,
Of times yet to come
Sky and sea
mirror each other.
The sea becomes what the sky cannot—
waves like clouds
dancing in sunlight.

To that place
I fled from—
I now return
with a half-smile,

Spring welcomes the year's first snow,
like a memory out of season.

Our stories of that time—
Now we sit leisurely and enjoy the days,
And in the stillness that brightens with clarity,
We engrave white names
into the stillness of snow,
and in the breath and names
they left behind,
old stories
come back to life.

The Ferry Dreams of the Taegeuk Bridge

The ferryboat of Sokcho—
facing the elders from the North,
a stop clock marks
a single voice
of those who live the present.

Every minute before noon,
cherished,
they endured with dependence
overcame with will
sat on chairs
and entrusted the seasons to time.

That infants must one day
face old age—
such is the law
of flowing time.

The truth
we wished to deny,
the reality
we must now accept—

the current of time
moves alongside
the waves of change.

For a moment,
we simply held on.

Beneath the crimson Seorak Bridge,
tears were shed.

Upon the blue Geumgang Bridge,
eyes dreamed anew.

Within the Taeguk Bridge,
adorned with mugunghwa and peonies,
cradled in the arms
of my father's embrace.

The Embrace of a Mother Whale Anchored on the ROKS Ulsan

The tenderness below,

the longing above—

always held in quiet suspension.

The deep echo of sonar

challenges the sea

to a solitary duel.

Blades of waves,

sharp enough to cut—

on the pointed edge

shines the breath

of a mother whale.

Within that ripple,

time holds its breath.

New lives follow, powerful,

while the great pine trees

align their limbs

to form a puzzle

just for them.

The dragon settles
upon jagged rocks—
blanketed by lullabies
it once whispered.

After a long, dark tunnel,
a flawless landing unfolds,
and the suspended switch
at last powers down.

A summer downpour passed—
and in its wake,
the radiant life we lost
has returned
to its rightful time.

International Arirang

Upon the round Earth,
strapped to countless steps,
we buckle our belts.

The erosion of weakness
is a universal truth,
as imperfect beings,
our eyes meet—
with hope.

Not a matter of change,
but a deepening authenticity—
to be ourselves.
a dignified, majestic movement,
the "International Arirang" we dance together.

As rivers flow
and lakes remain still,
the beautiful circle of life
unfolds once more.

We Walked the Map Together

Beneath the unfamiliar sky of Australia,
there were days
when glances led the way
before words ever did.

Maps folded,
time scattered—
yet the sunlight of those days
still rests in our bags.

When distant seasons bloom again
outside my window,
we grasp the winds of Europe
and step into the alleys of Korea.

Even as our steps slow,
even in silence,
your stride quietly waited for mine.

We trace each other
across the same map,
engraving our names, into shared paths—
so delicate, so precious.

The Desert Moon
That Reflected the Little Prince

A thirsty elephant,
unable to find the oasis,
hides beneath
a shaded hat.

The Little Prince, weary
on the steep dune of dusk,
leans into starlight
for comfort.

The barren desert is
merely silent.
A distant rose, watching,
sends her petals
on a falling star
to speak to the sand.

The wind stills.
And the desert
mirrors a quiet moon.
Reflected in that moon,
the Little Prince's tears

become an oasis—

from the snake's shed skin,

an elephant is born.

The scent of the rose he once tamed and forgot

returns at journey's end—

and in a single sip

beneath the desert moon,

invisible memories

take form

and ride the stars.

Spasiba(Спасибо)

Tears of the Koryo-saram
reflected in the river's surface,
the abundance it fed into the plains—
but the Balhae I met in Primorsky Krai
was shaped in black ash.

The blood-bound kinship remains steadfast and eternal,
   Yet even the northern skies of the peninsula
deny even the birds.

This peninsula named Korea
casts the Trans-Siberian Railway
into a restless wandering.

When will we wear the ring
on the Silk Road's artery?

In place of that ring,
we wore one of circular longing,
decorated not with gems
but the uniform expression

of ornate masks.

Side effects
of those who long for
the scent of humanity.

From small to great,
and great to small—
whether worn or removed,
it's but a difference in size.
Did we not laugh?

Upon the slick, cylindrical hues,
let us wear a slightly larger ring
and board the train together.

Two Crowns, Corona

Squirrels once drank their meals—
now they carry water
with cautious steps.

Do they mimic the passion
of Mexico's Corona beer?
Not heat—
but sting,
as your dizzying speed
spins the Earth in exhaustion.

On the hamster wheel
of bottled Corona,
the soft dilemma
takes flight.

Oh squirrels,
who halted
your frantic march on land!

Wings unfurl in darkness—
bats in transformation,
carrying the full weight

of both sacrifice
and sacrament.

A face-off
between irreconcilables—
you've tried so hard.

Because it's full, it can hear.
Because it's empty, it echoes.

Spring is still too far.
Return to hibernation,
and wait—
as creatures of shifting warmth—
for spring
in your own way.

Corona, duel of crowns—
wash the black-and-white masks
into the river.

Let us forge
a true alliance.

Post Coronaism
– In the Wake of the Pandemic

The Earth went dark—

were we clinging too tightly to what was worn?

Searching for space to let the new in,

it fled—

and found temporary shelter in our bodies.

A deep traumatic wound,

a massive turning point.

Was it karma?

Did we expect to escape?

Screens flashed finite numbers,

while the infinite taught us surrender.

But even in absence,

we grew the inner muscles to endure.

Through blurred clouds,

time passed with flawless precision.

The symmetry between sky and sea

is what the world owes us now.

The final moment, simpler than the start.

The storm cloud that once sought refuge

now tests the distance we've made.

To all the days we gave our all,
let us offer a passing glance—
not soaked in sorrow.
With a smile behind my loosened mask,
I remember—

That red flag of Venus, which once replaced
the bloodline of my homeland, in a stranger's embrace—
I fold away nostalgia, and rest in the arms of the Taegeuk.

The Purification of Fragments

Somewhere on this blue earth,
shards fly,
dappled and broken,
and the seeds of the planet
collapse in anguish.

Fragments shattered or cracked—
the residue around us,
green fading to grey,
wild things
howling in their fall.

The mountains of America and Australia
weep like fire.
Ugly locusts march through Africa,
and Earth's sorrow spills
across its wounds,
masking us in white.

These leftovers—
gathered, sorted,
recycled through hearts

made briefly whole.

Let us step back,
breathe
with the Earth.

Part 3

Like deep green leaves
stretching into growth,
you and I each rise—
one step at a time.

Buds turn to leaves,
memories to dreams.
The season turns its page
without a word.

In time,
the grown version of you
will find a way through.

It's Hard, but I Love You

In the clarity of drink,
I rest—
leaning into dependence.

Sounds that flew out—
they dissolve
the pale interrupters
floating in still water.

Words, once anchored,
settle like installed parts—
making calm
feel almost natural.

If known, it was understanding.
If unknown, it became misunderstanding.

Fresh flowers try to hold on,
but dry, bowing low,
they exhale their last breath of air.

I didn't want to ask,

but even the questions I longed to ask—

I wish to bury them
in this heavy heart,
withdraw the direction of my passion
for a while.

And become accustomed
to joy, anger, sorrow, and pleasure
without sound.

Indoor Cycling: Days on the Pedals

Wheels racing through air,
fatigue crushed beneath black tires—
the blood in my body
searches for a new path.

Eyes gleaming with breath and music,
I surrender to the bicycle's speed,
lay the weight of today on the pedals—
warriors of the everyday, all of us.

Beyond the mirror, I see myself,
a weary face, flushed red,
short of breath
yet eyes that refuse to give in.
Once again, I've outpaced myself.

Amid the creak of weary machines,
inner silence awakens,
and the burden of the day slowly descends.
Wordless comfort exchanged,
a bond stitched with sweat.

Each of us returns to our own night

with a heart grown stronger,

a spirit grown lighter—

leaving behind the promise of another day.

Temperature I

Is this moonlight in earthly darkness?
Or is it sunlight—
so bright
it cannot rise again?

In the parking lot,
a fluorescent light glows like sun.
We nod toward it—
together.

It flickers on when someone nears,
then rests again.

Like earphones
that block the outer noise—
through twin cords
a light flows upward,
gentle as body heat,
becoming another version of me,
sinking softly into my skin.

Temperature II

Temperatures
inside and out—
not quite free.

From the fickle wounds
of burns or frostbite.

From all that grows
harder to endure—
free yourself.

If something
can exist
with or without you,
then maybe—
it doesn't need to exist at all.

In the Late Night, Instead of the Sun

I liked the cool swallow—
Until I realized
it was because of your gaze
on the other side.

A one-legged pose—
how splendid it seemed.
It was just the lighting,
but your gulp
was a reservation
for what would follow.

Let it roll,
let it roll.

The colors I wear,
shimmering hues—
are chasing you.
What can I do?
Let me try that one spin too.

Who knows?

Perhaps I'll shine
following your light—

Even if
that moonlight
is only struggling
to imitate
the sun's fading edge.

Still—
aren't we shining together?

There's nothing
that does not shine.

The First Page of an Old Album

Like ground beetles
slipping in and out
through cracks in dry earth,
we come, we go.

Endless repetition
chasing the eternal—
weightless wanderers
face their difference.

So many tangles to unravel
before one line
can be found.

A memory misunderstood.
A photo perfectly clear.
Within it—
a time frozen in place.

On the opened page,
I pile up the longing I've hidden.
Like stars

shining unattended

they sit, quietly,

just like that.

Across the Thought-Bridge, Toward the Lighthouse

A bridge stretches
from the round cube.
Thoughts flow,
relations emerge,
new values take shape—
and the cube of thought
returns to us,
full.

In truth,
there is no such thing
as a minus in this world.
All things are added,
layered—

Every spin of the cube
reminds us:
Mother is our first home.
Even on nights of heavy thought,
stars still sparkle.
And in the morning,
sunlight pours in.

We, imperfect as we are,
lean on one another
to live.

All of us—
islands.

But all these islands
are connected by light,
threaded across the sea
by a lighthouse's beam.

A Holiday from
Joy, Anger, Sorrow, and Delight

Staring into the flames,

I looked up at the sky.

Suddenly,

something rushed in—

coloring the world.

But not my poem.

I couldn't add a single hue.

I filled the air

with the excuses

I despise the most.

What were circumstances to me

sounded like excuses

to you.

Tears and laughter,

barely hidden

behind a mask.

To show yourself,

to use your energy
while your self-worth is low—
what a difficult thing that is.

If you try to have everything,
you risk losing it all.

So I offer you
this nameless noun,
deep and still—
and hold you within it.

I seek not answers,
nor questions of the past.
Only
that we never feel
the need to ask.

Puppet Show

Gestures shift—
misaligned with the calm
of objective signs.

I move my hands
up and down
over the marionette
whose head shakes
as if dancing.

But the unchanged expression—
that same face—
asks whether to look up,
or look down
into the mismatched heart.

The wooden stick
attached to those puppet strings
wears glasses—
fashioned from light,
designed by projection,
glued together

with history.

As in youth,
when we changed clothes
each season,
we now invite
the finest things
into our lives,
and welcome them.

Wishing
is the first fruit.
The puppet,
with its stick-glasses,
bathes in light.

Summer,
in all its bright flourish,
awaits our arrival.

A new year begins
as we step forward

beneath piled-up clouds—

feet now feathered

with wings.

Hypnosis

Like a quiet dawn-blooming flower,
night gifts morning
intentionally—
as hope.

An artificial bloom
can never replace
a real one,
but still—
it offers color
and a smile.

The scent
left on the hand
that gave the flower
draws a vase
with a flower-butterfly.

Let it grow wings—
and fly
from night
to morning.

The Lost Shooting Star

A light,
clear in meaning—
lost in an instant.
Words scatter in the empty sky.

The care that tried to listen,
the starlight of empathy—

Now trails like a long tail,
falling
as a shooting star.

On the same day,
within the same hour—
something once shining
wanted to become
something more.

That brilliant moment
now floats in the air,
smaller
than a tear.

Confession

In the quiet of night,
a guest called "tear"
comes to visit.

"You feel better now,
after showing yourself?"
"It must've been hard,
holding it in so long."

Yes—
I accept you.

Let it flow.
Let me flow.

"I'm sorry,"
I whisper,
holding you
from behind—
then stop.
Let us not become
rain in this silence.

Sitting on the Stump

In hurried steps
I left behind
memories once white—
now lost,
now distant.

Where did
all those folktales go?

The stories inside
have worn thin,
left ragged
by the harshness of the outside.

There's nothing
I truly know—
and nothing
the world can say
is truly certain.

Passionate moments
bring us to many things.

But again and again,
I return
to the chair
I once passed,
believing I owned
what I merely encountered.

Oh, discarded memories—
once pushed away—
what kind of days
are you making now?

Han Kang author

I came to visit,
just once in a while—
but now the village
is far too crowded.

Out of breath,
I came running
to find my friend—
but the game
of hide-and-seek
has already begun.

I leave behind
my humming alleyway,
startled
by lights brighter than the sun,
flickering and loud.

I hide.

One day,
I hope to visit

my friend's house again—
no need to knock—
when quiet moonlight
falls upon the door.

Still,
I'm deeply grateful.

For you—
for everyone—
just being there.

Inside Out

Emotion melts into silence—
until existence itself disappears
Loss of presence,
becomes a storm cloud's tear.

Between passion and stillness,
we must lay down
courtesy and coexistence—
not out of defeat,
but release.

Eyes, hollow and distant,
wear shoes,
ride translucent vehicles,
and hum
forgotten songs.

Symbols too sacred
to be heard
or approached.

And yet—

the night sky

shone so brightly.

A Song for You

Even if paused,
a dream stirs,
like a sprout meeting the world
for the first time.

Dreams shift direction,
but like an infant
grasping its mother's hand—
they remain tender.

Like blood formed
from unseen bone,
the compass, though invisible,
points in every direction
you'll need.

The steady tick of a clock
will lead you there—
will applaud you.

Everyone can,
but not just anyone does.

Everyone might become,
but not all become.

Even in idle,
a dream that dreams
hands its key
to the dream
that still wants to be.

I Hope

Perched on a crossbar,
between lined boxes of thought,
love nestles—
and in that chest,
hope rises, yet collides.

In the brush of wind,
we breathe a wealth
not burdened by poverty of heart.

But kindness too much
feels suspect.
Did we, in doubt, hand over a blank check
to "what if"?

You know the seasons
first; one must
discipline the self.
If you wish to change the world,
let yourself
be changed.

In a sea,

perhaps wide yet shallow,
I long to sail—
narrow, but deep—
with great care,
and purpose.

To train the body through experience—
a quiet longing.
But when those boxes vanish
from view,
I sit on his shoulder,
and turn toward
a familiar sound.

Hope rises,
but again
it collides.

The lingering hues of the body
just glance
toward sound again,
and once more—
the boxes reappear.

Softly, Vienna

At first,
it was just a desk,
a blackboard,
and a distance beyond them.

The noise of protest
dissolved in sips of Vienna coffee;
the gaze of the audience
was nothing but thirst for learning.

After long nights of silent weeping,
mornings began with smiles
following the sun—
and on those repetitive days,
a glance
left chocolate atop Vienna coffee.

Tissues, once silently weeping,
wiped it away—
and with quiet, gentle smiles,
approached.
Soundless voices

offered silent encouragement,
placing a hand on the shoulder—

as if something once lost
had been found again.

Peace of the Golden Mean

Bearing the heavy weight
of this body,
I find myself fixed
in a sightline
so familiar
it feels strange.

I realize now—
in June—
how short a year truly is.

The seesaw play of
dream and pain
it rises, it falls
like a game of
hide-and-seek,
with moderation.

The seesaw I ride,
facing myself,
bows its head.

To preserve

what was passed down,

I stretch my toes forward—

reach for the truth

of Havruta,

and hold it to my heart.

Not What's Hot, But What's Warm

Wishes born from fear
rarely come true.

And so we continue
the rhythm of routine—
choosing
what to hold,
and what to let go.

A blank page
offers infinite space,
a playground
for all that could be.

Yet—
so many names
already etched in ink
grow anxious
if they do not change.

Because when I try to be strong,
others feel safe.

So I let the rain
walk across my face,
dimples forming
in small pools of cool.

A life that has passed through reflection
grows more colorful.

The simplest things endure.
So I choose
not what's hot—
but what's warm.

And an old dream, now peaceful,
returns to ask:

| Commentary |

Embracing the World, Painting a Vast Landscape of Poetry

Lee Seungha Poet, Chung Ang University Professor

What sets poet Suna, Jang apart from many other poets in Korea is her remarkably unique background. Her poetic journey has not been confined to the southern half of the Korean peninsula. This, in itself, is a significant asset. Having majored in both English and Korean literature during her undergraduate and graduate studies, she went on to study and work in Australia. After returning to Korea, she taught TOEIC to university students at institutions such as Dankook and Yongin University. From 2013 onward, she actively participated in various international literary events, working simultaneously as an interpreter and host. She also served as an external relations committee member for the Korean Writers' Association and as secretary-general for the Gyeonggi Province branch of the Korean PEN Center.

There was a period of roughly four years when poet Suna, Jang stage shifted to Vietnam. She was a journalist for a Korean magazine, Xin Chao Vietnam. She taught Korean at high schools, universities, and the Kanata Korean Language Institute in Hanoi. If it weren't for the outbreak of the COVID-19 pandemic, she may have remained there even longer. She has serialized English poems in Multicultural Daily, and her previous poetry collections, like the one in hand, are bilingual editions in Korean and English.

I begin with her biography for a reason: to better understand the poetry of Suna Jang, one must first contemplate the path she has walked.

In 1938, during the Japanese colonial period, the young poet Seo Jeong-ju wrote a poem titled "The Sea" for the magazine Sahae Gongron. He was twenty-three. This colonial-born intellectual cried out to his peers and juniors:

"Forget your father,
Forget your mother,
Forget your siblings, relatives, and friends,
And finally forget your beloved.

Go to Alaska, or to Arabia, or to America, or to Africa,
Or sink—sink—sink!"

He urged them not to stew in frustration on this narrow peninsula but to cast themselves out into the vast world and pursue their dreams. Perhaps his travels around the world in his later years were a way of fulfilling the dreams he could not realize in his youth.

Now let us turn to the poetry of Suna Jang:

>Beyond the window, at the runway's end,
>the familiar ground slowly fades.
>
>In my bag, an old goodbye,
>in my heart,
>a story unfinished.
>
>Those ties of time—
>linger at the dawn of departure,
>then vanish
>under the roar of ascent.
>
>Like the plane ticket in my hand,
>everything was but a page of a journey.
>
>Like the plane soaring through the sky,
>I carry myself—
>I hold my own hand.

Glancing back
through the airport glass wall,
my transparent reflection
promises the next sky to be.

The departure—home usually forgotten
has now
taught me to cherish
what remains—
and to love it all the more.
—from "The airport, Bonds Beyond Measure"

Anyone who has ever flown overseas, especially those who have lived abroad for any time, will resonate deeply with this poem. One's future seems to hang by the thread of a passport and a single flight ticket. You must venture into the unknown, speak in unfamiliar tongues, and meet strangers who do not understand you.

The line:

"Like the plane soaring through the sky,
I carry myself,
I hold my own hand."

reminds us that once airborne, the only person we can

truly rely on is ourselves.

Traveling abroad sparks dreams. The dream to once again board a plane and send oneself into the unknown. Some revisit places they've been, others always seek something new—but regardless, travel is our most viable escape from the hamster-wheel of daily life.

Her time in Australia is reimagined in this poem:

> Beneath the unfamiliar sky of Australia,
> there were days
> when glances led the way
> before words ever did.

> Maps folded,
> time scattered—
> yet the sunlight of those days
> still rests in our bags.

> When distant seasons bloom again
> outside my window,
> we grasp the winds of Europe
> and step into the alleys of Korea.

> Even as our steps slow,

even in silence,

your stride quietly waited for mine.

We trace each other

across the same map,

engraving our names, into shared paths—

so delicate, so precious.

—from "We Walked the Map Together"

Australia, nearly on the opposite side of the earth, is a continent in itself. South Korea, a small divided peninsula, is dwarfed in comparison—and only two-fifths of it is accessible. Landing in English-speaking Australia, the poet bravely embraced days when "gazes opened paths before words could."

Later, she writes:

"we grasp the winds of Europe / and step into the alleys of Korea."

"Even as our steps slow / even in silence, / your stride quietly waited for mine."

These lines portray a deeply human connection— between the poet and the other—across the vastness of the globe. "We trace each other across the same map," engraving a shared presence into the world. There is hardly a place today where Koreans are absent—whether first-generation immigrants or descendants born abroad. The song that unites them is Arirang.

> Upon the round Earth,
> strapped to countless steps,
> we buckle our belts.
>
> The erosion of weakness
> is a universal truth,
> as imperfect beings,
> our eyes meet—
> with hope
>
> Not a matter of change,
> but a deepening authenticity—
> to be ourselves.
> a dignified, majestic movement,
> the "International Arirang" we dance together.
>
> As rivers flow
> and lakes remain still,
> the beautiful circle of life

unfolds once more.

—from "International Arirang"

Arirang is no longer a song sung only by Koreans. It has become a song of shared resonance, something even foreigners hum along to. "as imperfect beings / our eyes meet / with hope"—therein lies the heart-to-heart communion that occurs through song. "Not a matter of change, / but a deepening authenticity— to be ourselves / a dignified, majestic movement, / the 'International Arirang' we dance together"—it is no longer just a Korean folk song. It has become an "International Arirang."

One of the poems bears a Russian title, likely born from a journey to the northern reaches beyond the Tumen River. Spasibo (спасибо)—pronounced "spasiba" in Russian—means thank you.

> Tears of the Koryo-saram
> reflected in the river's surface,
> the abundance it fed into the plains—
> but the Balhae I met in Primorsky Krai
> was shaped in black ash.
>
> The blood-bound kinship remains steadfast and eternal,

Yet even the northern skies of the peninsula
deny even the birds.

This peninsula named Korea
casts the Trans-Siberian Railway
into a restless wandering.

When will we wear the ring
on the Silk Road's artery?

In place of that ring,
we wore one of circular longing,
decorated not with gems
but the uniform expression
of ornate masks.

Side effects
of those who long for
the scent of humanity.

From small to great,
and great to small—
whether worn or removed,
it's but a difference in size.
Did we not laugh?

> Upon the slick, cylindrical hues,
> let us wear a slightly larger ring
> and board the train together.
> —from "Spasiba(Спасибо)"

Ah—when will we be able to board the Trans-Siberian Railway departing from Busan? As the poet asks, "When will we wear the ring / on the Silk Road's artery?" Balhae was once our ancestors' kingdom. Primorsky Krai was once our territory. Hyecho, the Buddhist monk, traveled the Silk Road as early as the 8th century. In that journey, the poet beheld the tears of the Koryo-saram. The final lines—"Let us wear a slightly larger ring / and board the train together"—resonate with the interpreter's longing for reconciliation and reunification.

The poet has lived abroad, traveled widely, taught English to Koreans and Korean to foreigners. All these experiences deepened one thing above all: a yearning for "Korea." Should we call it the land of our ancestors, or the motherland ? Why does this land feel so achingly dear when we're away? They say you become a patriot when you live abroad—no truer words. Upon returning to Korea, everything feels familiar, everything is comforting. And yet, the reality of division is felt even more sharply.

The ferryboat of Sokcho—
facing the elders from the North,
a stop clock marks
a single voice
of those who live the present.

Every minute before noon,
cherished,
they endured with dependence
overcame with will
sat on chairs
and entrusted the seasons to time.

That infants must one day
face old age—
such is the law
of flowing time.
 —from the first half of "The Ferry Dreams of the Taegeuk Bridge"

The displaced—known as the "38 Line Wanderers"—had difficulty settling into southern society. Wherever one goes, immigrants are often treated as outsiders. For those unfamiliar with Sokcho's gaetbae, a brief explanation:

it is a cable ferry connecting Abai Village in Cheongho-dong to downtown Sokcho. During the Korean War, refugees from Hamgyong Province created a northern enclave here, unable to return to their homeland. But the village was separated from the city center, prompting the birth of the ferry—a small wooden boat that offered a direct route across. Before it, people had to go the long way around. With dwindling use and economic strain, the village residents gave up operations, and as of May 1st last year, the Sokcho City Facilities Management Corporation took over for five years. The poet's dream, and that of the displaced, is rendered here:

> The truth
> we wished to deny,
> the reality
> we must now accept—
> the current of time
> moves alongside
> the waves of change.
>
> For a moment,
> we simply held on.
>
>
> Beneath the crimson Seorak Bridge,

tears were shed.

Upon the blue Geumgang Bridge,
eyes dreamed anew.

Within the Taeguk Bridge,
adorned with mugunghwa and peonies,
cradled in the arms
of my father's embrace.
—from the second half of "The Ferry Dreams of the Taegeuk Bridge"

If one were to ride the ferry upon returning from life abroad, the pain of division would strike with unbearable clarity. A South Korean passport grants access to nearly every country in the world—except just beyond the ceasefire line. Across that forbidden border live parents, siblings, relatives, childhood friends.

In an Empty Space
Had there been even the slightest possibility granted,
Though hopes born of anxiety may not come true,
An earnest prayer never falls to the ground.
Thus, the hand hesitates over what was left behind

Relief upon descent

And relief upon ascent

They meet,

They speak—

Of times past,

Of times yet to come

Sky and sea

mirror each other.

The sea becomes what the sky cannot—

waves like clouds

dancing in sunlight.

To that place

I fled from—

I now return

with a half-smile,

Spring welcomes the year's first snow,

like a memory out of season

Our stories of that time—

Now we sit leisurely and enjoy the days,

And in the stillness that brightens with clarity,

We engrave white names

into the stillness of snow,

and in the breath and names

> they left behind,
> old stories
> come back to life.
> —from "A Jeogori Stitched into a White Áo dài"

Korea and Vietnam once faced each other with pointed guns. But since opening diplomatic ties in 1992, trade exports have steadily increased year after year. With Coach Park Hang-seo having led the Vietnamese national football team for five years and four months, the relationship between the two countries has grown ever closer. What is past cannot be changed; it is the time ahead that matters.

> One step into shelter,
> after a long, slow journey,
> I come home—
> —final lines of "Home"

> When night falls again,
> Into the empty house where you've become a stranger,
> I quietly hide
> My anxious heart.
> —full text of "Hide and Seek"

> Even in the worldly life

Of strangers walking ahead of us,

There seemed to be few tears left to shed.

—opening stanza of "Self-Respect, Self-Compassion"

Memory may be

A survival mechanism

For the assurance of a safe future.

Even if that function fades,

One can still live

On happy memories alone.

—three stanza of "Testimony of Memory"

Such is the poet: she would at times clearly recall long-past events through the circuits of memory. While teaching Hangul and English, she would have more deeply realized her identity as a Korean. But whether it be through the body's travel or the soul's wandering, life inevitably returns us to home. Why else were phrases like life's path (人生行路) and life's drift (人生流轉) created? The end of all roads is always home.

Now, since poet Jang Suna has contemplated her own act of writing poetry, let us turn to some of her poems related to that introspection.

> On a night lit by moonlight,
>
> Leaning on the Milky Way,
>
> She transfers the heart
>
> That concealment through implication veils,
>
> And prepares
>
> A gift of language.
>
> —final lines of "Autobiography of a Poet"

The most important poetic phrase here is "implication (含蓄)." Poetry, she suggests, is implication itself. On a moonlit night, the Milky Way as seen from Earth may not appear all that vivid. But what of it? If she is "transferring the heart / that concealment through implication veils / and preparing a gift of language," then we can look forward to her forthcoming fourth poetry collection.

Notably, her poetry contains neither lengthy nor prose poems. This is because, to her, such forms are not born of poetic spirit, but of a prose mindset.

> Long poems
>
> Layered in thick clothes,
>
> Now walk
>
> The summer shore.

> Shortened lines
> Changed into light garments,
> Now splash about
> With buoyant steps.
>
> Not the kind of knot
> Unraveled by extreme pressure,
> But rather—
>
> A sip of still water
> Drawn from a long journey—
> That is the wish.
>
> —full text of "A Prayer Toward Poetry"

Her once-lengthy poems, now "layered in thick clothes / walk the summer shore"—form and content have long fallen out of balance. Such poems are now rampant. But the poet now chooses to splash about with light steps.

So she hopes her poetry will be "not the kind of knot / that unravels by extreme pressure / but rather… / a sip of still water / drawn from a long journey." She believes this is poetry's true function.

"Who is not a poet / before their own life?" (from

"Entwined Paths")—this line holds a truth earned from two decades of writing poetry. Poetry, ultimately, is the "quietest language." Poet Jang Suna must have discovered this truth at the sharp intersection of Korean and foreign languages—through her journeys abroad, and through her lived experiences abroad.

> On days when words fall short,
> Tears speak first,
> In place of lips.
>
> More quietly
> Than any words,
> They seek to heal.
> —full text of "The Quietest Language"

Having released her third poetry collection in her twentieth year since debut, she seems now to have settled both in body and spirit. It is with great anticipation that we look forward to the deluge of new meanings that are sure to pour forth like monsoon rains in her poetry's next season.

| English Editing Review |

Between the Lines, an Enduring Heart Remains

English Poem Editor,
Jonathan Sheerin from the USA.

Poetry itself can be a beautiful exploration of the things we hold in our hearts, minds, and souls. In life, we go through countless changes and challenges, but also moments of stillness, reflection, and revelation. I believe Ms. Jang's third book of poetry, (The Airport, Bonds Beyond Measure) beautifully weaves together personal introspection with universal truths about love, loss, memory, and transformation. Her poems move gracefully between moments of deep reflection and simple, poignant observations about the world and the human experience.

What makes Ms. Jang's work especially powerful is her ability not only to express herself, but to gently guide the reader into exploring their own heart, memories, and dreams. Her writing invites us into quiet spaces of contemplation—sometimes intimate, sometimes expansive—yet always sincere. There is something truly meaningful and magical about the way she captures the ordinary and makes it feel sacred.

It was a great honor to assist Ms. Jang with the English translation of this remarkable poetry collection. While editing the English poems she translated together, her work was not just a linguistic task, but a deeply emotional and cultural experience. These English translations open the door for a wider audience to experience the emotional richness of Korean poetry. Her poems are more than just beautiful words on a page—they are lived experiences, tenderly crafted and generously shared.

Through her poetry, Ms. Jang guides us on a journey— through the seasons of life, the echoes of memory, and the connections that endure even after time has passed. During my time working with her poems, I found myself on a journey of my own. Her work reminded me of the importance of meeting life with an open, expansive heart—even in a world so often dominated by logic, calculation, and uncertainty.

In this way, I believe Ms. Jang seeks to convey that grace, love, and hope are not abstract ideals, but ever-present forces that carry us forward. No matter the pain or sorrow the sun is still shining in the sky. Sometimes it takes courage to choose happiness. Through her poetry, she shows us that even in moments of loss or solitude, our shared capacity to love is the thread that binds us all—across time, language, and experience.

That, I believe, is the true essence of her poetry: a quiet, enduring reminder that we are all connected. I am very grateful to have the opportunity to work with Ms. Jang helping to edit her English translations of her poems.

베트남어 편

베트남어 번역_진수연 TRẦN THỊ XUYẾN
Hanoi University of Industry 졸업
International Graduate School of Language Education 석사 최우수 졸업

베트남어 번역 감수_레휘 콰 Lê Huy Khoa
베트남 Kanata가나다어학당 원장
박항서 축구감독 전담통역사 역임
한국어-베트남어 사전 편찬

베트남어 번역 진수연TRẦN THỊ XUYẾN

| Lời nói đầu |

Trong hai chữ "Thời gian và Nhân duyên"
ẩn chứa bao gương mặt, bao khoảnh khắc từng ghé qua
– rồi ở lại
khi tôi bước qua một dòng sông thời gian
Có những mối nhân duyên ghé qua như mùa trôi ngang,
Cũng có những mối nhân duyên còn ở lại mãi,
dạo bước qua những trang sách cuộc đời của chính tôi.
Tập thơ này là ký ức về những cái tên tôi muốn quên mà không thể,
là cảm xúc chẳng hề xa dù cách xa ngàn dặm,
là sự lưu dấu hành trình tôi khám phá và tìm lại con người thật của chính mình.

Khi viết và dịch những bài thơ này bằng tiếng Hàn và tiếng Anh, tôi đã nhìn lại ký ức của mình bằng đôi mắt của một người xa lạ.

Đó không chỉ là một sự chuyển đổi ngôn ngữ đơn thuần,

mà là hành trình khám phá một chiều sâu khác của tâm hồn mình.

Quá trình ấy giống như việc hát lại nỗi buồn quen thuộc bằng một ngôn ngữ mới,

với hy vọng bản nhạc ấy sẽ an ủi chính tôi cũng như một ai đó.

Tôi mong rằng khi bạn đọc tập thơ này,

một mùi hương mùa cũ, một mối nhân duyên xưa sẽ nở lại

và nhẹ nhàng gõ cửa trái tim bạn.

Mối nhân duyên ấy

sẽ khiến ngày hôm nay của bạn thêm phần ấm áp.
Cuộc sống có lúc khiến ta chông chênh
nhưng chính sự ấm áp bé nhỏ ấy
cuối cùng sẽ đưa ta trở về cạnh bên một người nào đó.

Tôi hy vọng tập thơ này
sẽ nhẹ nhàng gọi mùa cũ về cho ai đó,
hoặc như một dấu nghỉ lặng lẽ xoa dịu lòng một ai đó
ngay khoảnh khắc này.
Hãy dành tặng thời gian một chút thời gian.

Áo dài trắng vá Jeogori
(Phần áo trên của Hanbok)

Trong không gian trống rỗng,
nếu được ban một cơ hội – dù nhỏ
mong cầu hời hợt có thể tan đi,
nhưng nguyện ước chân thành ắt sẽ được hồi âm
và tôi ngập ngừng bàn tay
trước những điều mình từng bỏ lỡ.

Bình yên - khi lặng xuống,
bình yên - khi trào dâng,
Chúng chạm nhau,
trò chuyện
về những ngày đã qua
và những ngày chưa tới.

Bầu trời – cũng một sắc, ngỡ hóa biển
Biển có sóng – thứ mà trời không có,
bắt chước mây,
khiêu vũ dưới nắng vàng.
Nơi tôi từng chạy trốn
giờ chào tôi bằng gương mặt hân hoan,
giữa trời xuân – đón tuyết đầu mùa.

Câu chuyện năm xưa của chúng ta
giờ đây thong thả lặng, tận hưởng từng ngày,
càng tĩnh lặng, càng trong sáng –
nơi ấy tôi khắc lên những cái tên trắng tinh.

Mỗi hơi thở, tên gọi họ thốt ra
những chuyện cũ lại lặng lẽ ùa về.

Dấu lặng

Đừng phơi điều sâu kín
chongười chưa từng chạm đáy cuộc đời.

Những lời hứa
viết trên khung cửa sổ
bằng hơi thở – tận từ đáy lòng,
tan theo giọt mưa
đọng dưới mái hiên.

Nhưng đôi khi,
vết nhòa ấy
hóathànhđiều quý giá
giữa hai người..

Trên đời, làm gì có rạch ròi?
Đang vui – có thể buồn,
đangbuồn – có thể cười.

Tôi bỗng dần yêu
nhữngđêmlầntìmkýứcthấtlạc,
Khi tâm lặng
ánh nhìn cũng dịu lại.

Tiếng mưa
bậu bên khung cửa
lộp bộp - đánh thức ta.

Sân bay, Thời gian, Nhân duyên

Cuối đường băng ngoài khung cửa sổ,
mảnh đất quen thuộc dần xa khuất.
Trong vali - lời tạm biệt xưa cũ,
Trong lòng - câu chuyện chưa hồi kết

Thời gian ấy, nhân duyên ấy
đứng lặng nơi ngưỡng cửa phi trường
chôn vùi vào tiếng cất cánh của những chuyến bay
Như tấm vé trên tay,
tất cả chỉ như hành trình của một mảnh giấy

Như máy bay xé mây ngang trời,
tôi mang theo chính mình
tự nắm lấy tay mình.

Ngoái đầu nhìn lại
qua vách kính trong suốt
là hình bóng tôi
đang hẹn với bầu trời khác

Ra đi để quên,
giờ đây

lại khiến ta yêu hơn
những gì còn sót lại.

Thời gian, Nhân duyên

Khoảng cách và thời gian
Mối quan hệ bản chất chẳng liên quan,
chỉ lặng lẽ tích tụ từng phần, từng mảnh,
âm thầm nhân lên nỗi nhớ.

Nỗi nhớ dịu dàng của một tình yêu từng có,
con đường vòng ta từng nhận lấy tình thương.
Nơi ánh nhìn dừng lại,
là miền du hành chớp nhoáng – một điểm cắt ngắn ngủi chẳng hề song song

Ở hành trình chẳng dễ dàng ấy,
bằng cả ánh mắt và lời nói dịu dàng,
là những buổi phát sóng trực tiếp đồng hành quý giá,
cùng những buổi chiếu lại.

Cuộc gặp gỡ không tỉ lệ với thời gian,
những lời nói từng thái quá dưới bỏ bọc gọi là "lần đầu tiên"
giống như giấy gói cho một món quà lộng lẫy.

Dù đếm bao lần những vòng lặp tái sinh

những con số đã bỏ cuộc giữa hữu hạn
thì vẫn còn đó
một đứa trẻ mồ côi – ngôn từ đi lạc vào vô cùng.

Tàn dư của ký ức còn sót lại,
tôi nâng niu chút năng lượng nhỏ nhoi
để bước vào một năm an dưỡng —
nơi trái tim được phép nghỉ ngơi.

Rồi mọi chuyện sẽ qua

Ký ức – lạ thay - luôn gắn với nước mắt.
những khoảnh khắc gần gũi thì ngắn ngủi,
mà lúc mất nhau, xa dần – lại dài hơn.
hãy kéo thời gian như một đường chạy nước rút
để giải thoát bản thân khỏi tất cả những điều này.

Dẫu trước mặt ngổn ngang bao thử thách,
Chỉ cần giữ trái tim nguyên vẹn, từng bước vững vàng mà đi,
Rồi sẽ có bàn tay nào đó nâng ta dịu bớt niềm đau.
Biết đâu đấy, điều ta mơ – sẽ thành hiện thực?

Rồi thời gian sẽ trôi,
và một phiên bản trưởng thành hơn của bạn
sẽ tìm ra cách vượt qua tất cả.

Hiệu đính bản dịch tiếng Việt
Lê Huy Khoa từ Việt Nam

Trong suốt thời gian giảng dạy tiếng Hàn tại Việt Nam, thầy luôn mang trong tim mình một tình yêu sâu đậm dành cho đất nước Hàn Quốc và thi ca.

Giờ đây, tình yêu ấy đã nở hoa trong hình hài của một tập thơ, mang đến cho độc giả vẻ đẹp tinh tế của ngôn từ và dư âm dịu dàng của cuộc sống.

Sự ra đời của tập thơ này không chỉ đơn thuần là một dấu mốc xuất bản, mà còn là minh chứng quý báu cho tầm nhìn sâu sắc và trái tim nhân hậu của thầy – người luôn biết nhìn thế giới bằng ánh mắt của sự thấu hiểu và yêu thương.

Khi thì nhẹ như làn gió, khi thì ào ạt như cơn mưa mùa hạ. Mỗi bài thơ là một khoảnh khắc của đời sống – nơi niềm vui, nỗi buồn, tình yêu và những day dứt lặng thầm cùng hiện diện. Thơ không chỉ là ngôn từ, mà là nhịp tim, là hơi thở, là khoảng lặng để ta dừng lại, lắng nghe chính mình.

Hy vọng thông qua bài thơ này các bạn độc giả sẽ tìm thấy sự đồng cảm, chút an yên, và có khi – một tia sáng nhỏ trong lòng.